# Organizational Jazz

## Extraordinary Performance
## through
## Extraordinary Leadership

*This book is dedicated to each special member of
our families.
You give us joy, inspiration and
nurturing – always.*

David Gilhespy - of your permaculture values

    Earth Care
      People Care
        Surplus Share

        the "People Care" value reflects the spirit of this book

Acknowledgments

There are many fellow travellers on this journey and they include the many courageous "front line employees", managers and executives. We are grateful for the support, encouragement and the opportunities to travel with them. People who supported the journey and gave generously their time and thoughts on the change programmes include Peter Vaughton, Keith Hillier, Gary Langton, Ian Healey, Bob Frizell, Simon Linge, Louis Caruana, Bob McArdle, John Cleary, Mike Byrne, Ian Tunnecliffe, Hans Langendam, Chong-Jin Chong, Greg Waters, Rob Crawford, Mike O'Loughlin, Steve Wickham, Damien Marantelli, Rowena Smith, Alan Gageler, Graeme Fitzgerald, John Monoghan, Geoff Voigt, Daphne Hart, Bernie Cooper, Bronic Karcz, Andy Paton, Sean Winstone, Rob Elder, Peter MacLean, Susan Feeney, John Vickers, Paul Day, Barry Nicholls and the many thousands of participants in the workshops, who provided a rich and unique education for us. We also acknowledge all the unique individuals that we have met in our lives who have taught us how complex human systems are. We would like to acknowledge Jann Barker for her support over the years and Yvonne and Lindsay Quann from Karriview Lodge, for their generosity during the writing of this book. We are particularly indebted to Bob Dick and the late Fred Emery who have contributed to our learning over many years. Also, we are deeply indebted to Andrew Carter and his team for their insights and, the courage to do something extraordinary to achieve extraordinary tangible results. Lastly, thank you to Terry Thomas, Carolyn Gay and Barbara Ridyard, who reviewed drafts of this book.

David, Alma and Kathrine

# Organizational Jazz

## Extraordinary Performance through Extraordinary Leadership

David Napoli, Alma M. Whiteley and
Kathrine Selmer Johansen

Routledge
Taylor & Francis Group

LONDON AND NEW YORK

First published 2005 by Goshawk Publishing

Published in 2016
by Routledge
2 Park Square, Milton Park, Abingdon, Oxon OX14 4RN
711 Third Avenue, New York, NY, 10017, USA

*Routledge is an imprint of the Taylor & Francis Group, an informa business*

ISBN 13: 9780975771068 (pbk)


Napoli, David.
  Organizational jazz : extraordinary performance through
  extraordinary leadership.


  Rev. ed.
  Bibliography.
  Includes index.
  ISBN 0 9757710 6 X (pbk.)

  1. Leadership. 2. Management. 3. Business enterprises -
  Management. 4. Success in business. I. Whiteley, Alma M.
  II. Johansen, Kathrine S. III. Title.


  303.34

# TABLE OF CONTENTS

## CHAPTER 6

## CHAPTER 7

# Preface

# 'Organizational' Jazz

This book is a conversation and we start with a fun comment. It has been four years in the making and we have lived through many of the experiences we recount or make sense of. We are delighted to mention seminal authors but maintain that this book is not an academic text. Like the jazz metaphor we explain below, there is and always has been an underlying theme to our approach to organizational life. The theme is the people. The variety is the way people are constantly surprising us with their wisdom and energy. This book is for them, the people in the workplace who have shared with us their wisdom and understanding.

It is interesting that when we tell people the title of the book on which we are working, they hardly stop and think, before nodding. It seems so natural. Jazz as a metaphor, conjures stability in the tune and uncertainty in the improvisations. This is what we try to do also in this manager-as-leader practitioner book. From our experience, we blend theory and practical examples. We are privileged to bring stories of organizations that have gone beyond limited expectations by creating environments that endorse innovation and productivity whilst allowing people to work with dignity. What they deliver, as we see it is an improvised piece of 'organizational' jazz.

Jazz inspires creative musicians to improvise, yet work together with others in the orchestra. Improvising, even in general terms, is often not respected in organizations for various reasons. Often, there is the expectation that things really ought to be done to a certain way of thinking. This sort of thinking suggests that deviation from the normal is dangerous. This, we think, is very limiting. For us, beyond the "risks horizon" lies exciting possibilities.

Returning to music, the classics, although recorded in a structured manner for exact reproduction, have their roots in improvisation during original conception. Those that follow a set score, note for note, repeating the past over and over, undoubtedly produce beauty.

However, those crazy risqué jazz musicians can take the past and create further unlimited variations, giving colour and the unexpected quality of possibility to the underlying score. The conductor and orchestra 'master and followers' relationship is replaced in the jazz 'band' of people so that each learns from the other. They create inspiration not only for themselves, but engage those who listen in anticipation. Yet, they work within boundaries such as musical key, technical competence, melody line and tempo. To these they add spontaneity to achieve exciting and creative music beyond limitation.

This book is not an academic undertaking, although conventions of writing and referencing have been followed. It is a storybook, a series of thoughts and conversations between those engaged in organizational life and the authors (who include our storytellers). We have chosen to share our ideas and memories with the reader in the spirit of promoting conversation and innovative thinking.

Our ultimate aim is to promote organizations that enable people to not only create wealth for shareholders but for society at large and in a way that offers respect and dignity. We believe that to waste the resources of society is not acceptable and we hope to suggest ways in which resources, including human resources, are optimized. With new thinking it is possible that these ambitions may be achieved as we pass the management baton to the next generation.

We are keen to challenge some of the underlying beliefs that govern behaviour in organizations. The belief that we operate in a certain and predictable world is a fantasy that society can no longer afford. The belief that mankind can control its environment is a myth that has been thrust upon most of us from an early age. Such fantasies and myths are no longer helpful in building productive, satisfying and sustainable organizations.

Albert Einstein suggested that no problem could be solved by using the same thinking that created it. We need to search with new eyes and new ways of thinking. He also said that imagination is more important than knowledge, but just in case...we have brought you both.

We believe strongly that the success of an organisation usually depends on those working closest to the value-adding end of the business.

It is those employees and their immediate leaders, who seem to have the greatest impact on the success of an organization. They drive the pedals, they pull the levers and push the buttons and they deliver the service to the final customers. Ultimately, it is they who add value to their organizations' processes. Managers and others have a different job to do. They may be able to do little more than read the dials of performance but they can ease the way for those who depend on them for support and encouragement. They are responsible for providing leadership.

This book is directed mostly to those who drive the pedals, pull the levers, push the buttons and deliver the service to the customer. We also hope that it will provide insights for those responsible for creating environments where people not only can, but want to, release the discretionary energy that is always there, waiting to emerge. We are passionate about creating wealth for every organizational member and we invite you to join us in our journey.

# Chapter 1

## INTRODUCTION

The scene takes place in the mining industry somewhere in Australia. It is in the early hours of the morning, a time for thinking and philosophising. A group of workers, mates, are talking and thinking about life at work. They are musing about the never-ending mysteries of what goes on in the workplace, and in particular how managers never seem to hit the mark of mutual understanding.

*'It's as though we speak a different language on the job, and the strange thing is that when we all go for a beer, the problem disappears.'*

*'That's not my biggest problem, what bothers me is why managers rarely seem to do what they say they will do. They just don't walk the talk.'*

*'Yeah...and then when we ask them something, they always seem to hide something – how can they expect us to give our all when they don't share things with us?'*

*'Not only that'*, comes another response, *'managers always act as though someone – some unseen force – is pulling their strings. Reminds you of Star Trek.'*

*'That's true. I suppose they've got pressure on them too – and all those bloody stupid rules...'*

*'Rules, rules, rules, sometimes you feel so boxed in that you aren't sure that you should go 'you know where' without checking on a rule,'* sighed one of the group, an old timer.

*'The strange thing is,'* says one of the newcomers to the shift team, *'we seem so near and yet so far. These guys in management*

*are really decent people and yet they just don't get how we think and what we need.'*

*'And what's more,'* says his mate, *'I think they feel the same about us. If you ask me, we are all boxed in, and from what I can see, it can get very comfortable in these boxes. I haven't been here all that long but it all becomes so bloody boring. You're glad to get home and feel that you're something more than an extra set of arms and legs. At least your kids think that your brains are worth picking. What I would really like is help on how to make my work life and my home life similar in the things that matter. I don't want an imbalance between work and home as though one were the enemy. I want one to be a part of the other.'*

They stared morosely into their coffees and pondered on the double lives they seemed to live – one at work where they were boxed in, often of their own doing – and one where they could think for themselves, take a chance, make some mistakes and still come up smiling.

In another area of the factory, a group of managers are talking.

*'I honestly don't understand them. They're bickering and complaining about so many stupid things. I've tried to tell them what I know, but it seems like they just don't trust us.'*

*'Yeah, it's the same old thing. You try to do your best for them and they just want to keep on and on about the same old things.'*

*'You know, I asked for some help the other day with a break down, but do you think anyone wanted to stay back and help?'*

*'They're not a bad lot you know, my kids go to the same school as some of their children, so we meet sometimes outside of work. It's just that they're not enthusiastic. But how can we make it different for them?'*

We could peek in on such conversations all over Australia and not only in the mining industry. Almost since the first organizational forms and formats were invented, there has been a very visible 'us and them' way of thinking. It may be a bit unkind to call it 'managers think and workers do' as Fredrick Taylor[1], the famous scientific manager suggested, but we must admit that in deed if not in word, this is sometimes what we see.[2]

In this book, we are facing such problems head on. Basing ourselves in large organizations that have asked themselves the hard questions and gone on to do something about them in practice, we listen and learn as managers and workers tell us their stories. We will present them to you, the reader, to strike a chord with some of the experiences you have gained as you have gone through working life. Some of these may have kept you awake too, as you may have watched your best efforts dissolve into cynicism, resentment, or worst of all, apathy. As workers, you may have marvelled at how much of your talent and creative thinking has been untapped, seemingly unneeded. In fact you may not have even recognised that you had any particular talent if it was left to the workplace.

Following this introduction is a chapter we have called "The Dance and the Music". We identify the need to dance a new dance to the old music, working together within boundaries, however, departing from the ordinary or usual. We take a look at the nature and models of change and through this learn why identifying the nature of variables is so important in strategy, change and leadership. We present here some ideas and principles that scholars have contributed to our thinking.

When you leave this, you will meet the chapter on mechanistic management. We are fairly critical here as the lack of deep and fundamental criticism is something that this style of management has, perhaps, suffered from in the past. We maintain that some of the mechanisms we talk about such as rules, regulations, and procedures are necessary if not vital to keep organizations safe and legal. However, as you see in our 'yin' and 'yang' figures, too much 'mechanistics' inevitably leads to too little liberation of people to exercise their wisdom, understanding and individual/collective knowledge and experience.

---

[1] Taylor, F. W. (1911). *The Principles of Scientific Management.* New York, Harper & Row.
[2] Whiteley, A. (1995). *Managing Change: A core values approach.* Melbourne, MacMillan Education Australia Pty Ltd.

From chapter four, we take you to the transformational edge. In fact, we do no more than mirror the world as it is for most of us anyway. Thankful though we are to have some certainty, work premises, car parks, routines and so on, the 'inside' of organizational life is fraught with the unexpected. Sometimes this is a delight and sometimes a worry, but never is it as boring and controlled as the most avid mechanistic manager might believe. In chapter four, then, we talk about learning to lead and manage in a world that is far from certain, in which, for many things, there is far from any agreement. We owe a debt here to many writers and scholars who have helped us to translate theories of transformation in to practices such as the extraordinary leadership workshop, designed and facilitated by David (and we have all helped at times). It gives us pride to say that upward of five thousand people have attended the workshop which, in its full form, is a week-long residential. In this chapter, we introduce some terms from complexity theory and you will find them, referred to throughout the book, either as concepts or practices.

Chapter five is our 'reflection and making sense' chapter. Here, we outline the ideas and concepts first as they compare with the ones we have used in chapter three and then, in part two, the ones that are almost unnecessary in mechanistic management but come very much to the fore in extraordinary leadership. These are mostly relational and we use some of the metaphors and ideas from complexity theory to offset the trap of explaining an exciting future in the words and images of the past. As the famous philosopher, Wittgenstein, said 'we are prisoners in the cage of our language'. This is why you will meet terms like the strange attractor and fractals to project images of 'organizational magnet' and 'self similar but uniquely different behaviour' that these two terms portray.

Following the reflections chapter, we introduce the 'Extraordinary Leadership Program' we talked about earlier in the introduction. Words can not convey the experience of watching people work in a non-hierarchical environment where they gradually, over the week, 'find' resources, skills and talents that they did not know or even remotely suspect they had. The chapter describes the workshop itself, and we have persuaded David that it would not be too immodest to share just a few of the reactions and reflections of those who attended various workshops. For the mechanistic leader, the workshop might come under the heading of 'danger, whole people at work'.

One of the syndromes of the last twenty or so years is that of political correctness. It has not been OK for some time now to be considered as a poor corporate citizen whether this is inside or outside of the organization. This has resulted in many cases in declarations, in public and in the press such as 'people are our greatest asset'. Nice to hear, but do organizational structures and organizing practices bear scrutiny on this score? Does it matter and how would the manager/leader know? Stirred by one of these inspirational declarations in the press, and because only a few days before, workers were on strike not because of pay and conditions, but because they were not valued, the PATOP model was built. Basically this is a 'walk the talk' diagnostic model for leaders, teams and even individuals to check out the talk and the walk. Thanks to the devotion and encouragement of many PATOP users over the years, we bring you an extended version which also deals with strategic change.

Following PATOP we bring to you a summary of extraordinary leadership and then in Chapter 9 we provide a possible lens through which we may understand why the journey along the path of extraordinary leadership may be difficult for some people.

The remaining chapters are stories from organizations who have transformed themselves in an extraordinary way. In doing this, we hope to convince readers that however much of a 'mechanistic ceiling' is above them, it is possible to take people to (and over) the transformational edge. We hear stories about the life of uncertainty and far-from-agreement that to us is much more realistic than the 'fantasy' one of control. Interestingly, in liberating people and coping with diminished opportunity for control, the leaders, especially those who have been in the workshop, find that productivity goes up, whatever the constraints and uncontrollable variables.

More than anything, we hope that you will enjoy being with us, sharing our ideas and experiences.

# Notes

# THE DANCE AND THE MUSIC

Many managers are aware of the needs of the present and future. Pressures and problems are not only greater than ever before, but they are experiencing different problems. Their tried and tested solutions just don't seem to work anymore. The way we like to think of it is that managers are being asked to dance a new dance to the old music. It's here that we liken organizations to jazz players. They are working together, but improvising in ways that depart from the ordinary or usual, to deliver something new and exciting. Their music is eclectic, yet they are playing to the same tune.

In this chapter we are going to bring you some of the views of our favourite management scholars. In his book, 'Strategic Management & Organizational Dynamics', Ralph D. Stacey[3] provides a useful and intriguing lens through which possible options for organizations can be explored. We would also like to acknowledge scholars such as Meg Wheatley[4], the late Fred Emery[5], and Bob Dick[6], who we have quoted elsewhere as well as Stacey for their ideas and principles. These, presented with great scholarship, have contributed to our thinking. We add to their writings our experiences and ideas, focusing on the topic of strategic change.

Strategy, change and leadership go hand in hand. We believe that the ordinary methods of the past need to become the extraordinary ones of the future. We begin by looking at the nature of change.

---

[3] Stacey, R.D. (1996) *Strategic Management & Organizational Dynamics 2nd Ed.* London, Pitman.

[4] Wheatley, M.J. (1994) *Leadership and the New Science Learning about Organization from an Orderly Universe.* San Francisco, Berrett-Koehler.

[5] Emery, M., Ed. (1993) *Participative Design for Participative Democracy.* Canberra, Centre for Continuing Education, Australian National University.

[6] Dick, B. http://www.uq.net.au/~zzbdick/default.html

## Nature of Change

For Peter Senge[7] and his colleagues, people seeking change in organizations may use many different labels (as we ourselves often do) but essentially Senge captures the essence of change.

> [Organizations are] Trying to respond quickly to external changes and think more imaginatively about the future. They want better relationships with less game playing and more trust and openness. They want to unleash employees' natural talents and enthusiasm. They want to move genuinely close to their customers. Through all of this, they are striving to shape their destiny, and thereby achieve long-lasting financial success.

Many change writers and managers share some central ideas about what is involved when change happens. One is that change is really a feedback loop, and one that is not linear, but more resembling a series of interacting feedback loops, never still, always dynamic and coming in different guises.

For example, Senge talks about 'fear and anxiety' feedback loops, 'no help' feedback loops, 'not relevant' feedback loops, 'not enough time' feedback loops. Remember, these are all feeding back into the organizational system at varying times and with varying intensity. As he says succinctly, (p61) 'In any complex system like an organization, there is a myriad of forces and tensions seeking their own set-points, all trying to resolve one another – especially when you add in the various priorities and aspirations of the people involved'.

A famous organizational scholar, Mary-Jo Hatch[8] produces for us a rational model of the strategic change planning process. Although there are many components leading into the implementation stage, (external appraisal, threats and opportunities, key success factors, internal appraisal, strengths and weaknesses, distinctive competencies,

---

[7] Senge, P., Kleiner, A., Roberts, C., Ross, R., Roth, G., Smith, B. (1999) *The Dance of Change: The Challenges of Sustaining Momentum in Learning Organizations.* London, Nicholas Brealey, p5 and p105.
[8] Hatch, M. J. (1997) *Organization Theory. Modern, Symbolic, and Postmodern Perspectives.* New York, Oxford University Press.

impacts of social responsibility and managerial values) these are implicitly 'decidable' and flow in a logical sequence.

It is interesting that contrasting the complexity view proposed by Senge and the rational view described by Hatch, there are some things in common.

There is a need to find out what others inside and outside of the organization are doing; choices need to be made as to what to do with this information; implementation happens and impacts and consequences are fed back into the next strategic review.

So what is the difference between managing strategic change in a rational (and much easier) way and managing it under assumptions of (high) uncertainty and complexity? For this, it seems, we need to depart from purely rational thinking. (However, we argue later that there needs to be a rational element in the most complex thinking). We need to shift what Senge calls our mental model, mindset or special way of looking at the world. In a rational mindset, it is possible to imagine a fairly stable environment. You're fairly sure of the forces working for or against you and pressure to change is not continuous.

In a complex, highly uncertain mindset, you can look forward to the unexpected as a matter of course. People that do this put energy into the present which influences the future. They look at the possibilities that the present situation may hold. They find creative and innovative ways to move forward. People who don't accept uncertainty put energy into the past. When things do not work out as they did in the past, they hang on to feelings of disappointment and frustration. This comes in part from an underlying desire or need to control events (we'd all like to do that – but it's not useful in reality). It is not possible to apply well-tested solutions from your past experience unless all the variables are exactly the same in the future situation. You need to be constantly re-inventing and renewing, unlike the more stable situation where you have the time and ability to predict that which will allow you to proceed rationally. The rational journey focuses on balance, with equilibrium its desired end. The journey that takes in the future and all the complexities that come with it brings the need to adapt to constant changes. Life becomes quite unbalanced at times and it focuses more on the other end of the equilibrium continuum, usually called 'far from equilibrium' where change occurs. Although both seek equilibrium the journeys are quite different.

As in nature, even when things look chaotic, (and that is also a term, often associated with uncertainty and complexity) patterns do emerge. Patterns are what strategy is about. For survival we find people continually adjusting their strategies to the ever-changing circumstances presented by interacting feedback loops and incoming information. The interesting conclusion is that when people work together in organizations their behaviour impacts on others in unique and continually changing ways. Their interactions are non-linear in nature. In fact, it is the members of the organization that determine the way 'things are actually done'. We believe that there is a need to have a management function in order to cope with the surprise generated by this type of change. In other words, to make sure the organization does not become out of control. How often have you heard management express the need to 'get the place back on the rails'?

It is the organization's expectations of managers that often presents a problem. They are expected to make the organization predictable and stable by putting rules and systems in place. The expectation is that rules govern. To some extent they are designed to 'stand in' for managers. Logically speaking, if this were the case and if there were enough rules, there would be little need for managers. In real life, managers are needed. Because rules do not fit unique and changing circumstances, managers are needed to change or even bend the rules to ensure that the organization operates. It has always been intriguing to us that when the public sector unions want to inflict some pain on their employers they often apply a 'work to rules' tactic from their arsenal of industrial action. It is commonly understood that to 'work to rules' prevents the smooth running of a workplace.

It is interesting to observe that people seem to be obsessed with strategic management as an orderly and conformist process with certainty and predictability a fundamental aim.

Stacey[9] argues:

---

[9] Stacey, R.D. (1996) *Strategic Management & Organizational Dynamics 2nd Ed.* London, Pitman (p 22).

*...they keep losing sight of the fact that there are situations in which it is completely meaningless to talk about planning, or even shared intention as the process driving management action. It is therefore, in my view, a matter of great importance to go through the reasoning about the need for different management processes in different situations...*

Stacey is joined by Champy[10], who shows more optimism when he says

*Re-engineering, however, calls into continual question all the traditional hows and wherefores of these [management] processes and this questioning ...has unleashed a torrent of fresh thinking and acting on these topics.*

What becomes apparent from writers such as these and many more is that we need different types of decision-making and control strategies to meet different and unforeseen situations we encounter.

It is only when we think about our present state that we face the need to design our next action. We have to act in the present and with the knowledge that exists now. We need to be able to predict some of the consequences of our decision, *yet at the same time* recognise that there are many outcomes that cannot be known. Some of these outcomes may even escalate or surpass our imagined future – a realm of unimagined possibility. Stacey[11] draws attention to three different types of change that will be useful in developing the model of strategic leadership.

The first model of change is well known to us. Writers have various labels for it and Stacey[11] calls it 'closed change'.

**Closed change**

We were talking earlier about Hatch's description of a stable, in-equilibrium environment where prediction can occur and very often solutions to new circumstances are within the current experience. We

---

[10] Champy, J. (1995) *Reengineering management: The mandate for new leadership* London, Harper Collins (p117).
[11] Stacey, R.D. (1996) *Strategic Management & Organizational Dynamics 2nd Ed.* London, Pitman (p 23).

can all clearly say what has happened, why it happened, and what the consequences were. Obviously we can say with certainty what the impact will be if a particular decision is made. There is certainty about the outcome and there is widespread agreement about the consequences. A typical example comes from manufacturing, where it is widely understood what the consequences will be if one or more variables are changed within a stable production process.

In those circumstances we experience situations that are *close to certainty* and *close to agreement.*

Stacey[12] presents us with the concept of contained change and this has connotations of Mintzberg's[13] model of middle level uncertainty and complexity.

**Contained change**

This is a situation where the consequences of past actions are less clear and all that can be done is to speculate on what happened, the likely causes and the probable impact. It is usually accompanied by a statistical probability. For example, a manufacturer of roofing material may find it difficult to explain why one type of cladding sold more than others and will therefore find it difficult to predict which type of cladding will sell better in the future. However, market research and statistical information may provide some useful projections for short term forecasting only. Here, the cause is seen as approximate or statistical.

Contained change still has elements of being close to certainty and close to agreement. It differs from closed change in that it is not as certain and agreement is not as absolute.

Another example of this is in the hospitality industry. A seaside village draws more tourists in summer – it can be predicted with a fair amount of certainty that occupancy in the resort will decrease next winter.

---

[12] Stacey, R.D. (1996) *Strategic Management & Organizational Dynamics 2nd Ed.* London, Pitman (p 23).
[13] Mintzberg, H. (1990) The Design School: Reconsidering the Basic Premises of Strategic Management. Strategic Management Journal 11: 171-195.

The next concept produced by Stacey is that of open-ended change and this is conceptualized by Rosabeth Moss-Kanter[14] as innovative change. The central idea, as we see next is in direct contrast to a closed or contained situation.

## Open-ended change

This is where we do not know with any clarity some or all of the following; what caused the change, why the change occurred, and what the consequences will be. Obviously, there is no widespread agreement, with many reasons put forward for the change. In the roof-cladding example, a change in buying patterns could be the result of intensive advertising by competing producers. However, it could be (some may suggest) mismanagement within the company resulting in a decline in market share, whilst others suggest it could be unfair competition from imported products, and so on. Some see the change to be permanent while others see it as temporary. This is open-ended change. You can see from the various and competing suggestions that *far from agreement* and *far from certainty* is the case here.

Let's look at these concepts in a little more depth. What does it mean to be close to and far from certainty? Although we use Stacey's[15] terms, the concepts are well supported by other writers as well as in our own experience.

## Close to certainty

In situations where we are close to certainty there are clear links between cause and effect and the results of actions taken can be forecast with accuracy. Because of this, managers are reasonably clear about the problems they face and the opportunities available to them. There is little ambiguity and people resolve issues through rational debate or bargaining. People know what they are doing and will have decided what to do well before change occurs. When people are close to certainty it is relatively easy for them to reach

---

[14] Moss-Kanter, R. (1984) *The Change Masters: Innovation for Productivity in the American Corporation*, London, Allen and Unwin.
[15] Stacey, R.D. (1996) *Strategic Management & Organizational Dynamics 2nd Ed.* London, Pitman.

agreement with one another. As Hatch[16] points out, you can easily understand the internal and external impacts you face because you assume that things are relatively simple.

### Far from certainty

Far from certainty puts the manager in the opposite situation. She will face actions and events that are unexpected and have unknown consequences. A major difficulty here is to identify the problems that exist and the opportunities available. The problem of identifying the answers is not the issue. Rather, knowing what questions to ask becomes the focus of attention. The situation here is ambiguous and quite fuzzy.

When far from certainty we can expect conflict to occur about how to interpret what is going on and how to respond. As you saw in the case above, some people thought competition was the problem, others thought it was because of imported products and others still, internal mismanagement (In fact it could well be traces of all these and more). It is easy to see that rules, structure and solutions to problems that were developed from past experiences are of no use to us in this new state of uncertainty. If they did work we would find ourselves back in a state close to certainty and the problems would be easily solved.

When people are operating in conditions far from certainty, they rely more and more on the relationships that they have with each other. The dynamics of their interactions add to the complexity produced by all this uncertainty. Sometimes this complexity generates quite bizarre behaviour (Or is it only us?). You can see that the use of rational processes to deal with such situations can be quite inappropriate.

---

[16] Hatch, M. J. (1997) *Organization Theory. Modern, Symbolic, and Postmodern Perspectives.* New York, Oxford University Press.

**Some questions to ponder**

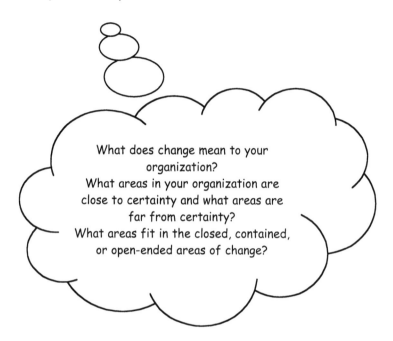

What does change mean to your
organization?
What areas in your organization are
close to certainty and what areas are
far from certainty?
What areas fit in the closed, contained,
or open-ended areas of change?

# Notes

# MECHANISTIC MANAGEMENT

Thinking and musing just before the book went to press, we had an idea of how to express our wish to have a *both/and* rather than an either/or approach to leadership. This chapter from necessity is critical about the whole mechanistic outlook, especially regarding people, but when we were chatting about this, we realized that we do need rational and mechanistic elements in organizations and some need more than others. How to portray this? We came up with the yin (feminine qualities) and yang (masculine qualities) idea where masculine (mechanistic and feminine (complex) elements combine to make up a whole (Figure 3.1). We liked the idea of the whole and then, within the whole, judgement can be made about how much yin and how much yang.

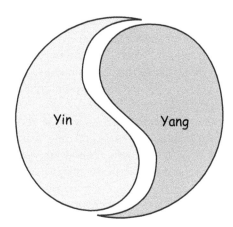

**Figure 3.1 Balance in the whole**

The reason we have embarked on the mission to break what we see as a stranglehold of the masculine, objective, rational way in which many organizations work is that they are not in balance as our next Figure 3.2 shows

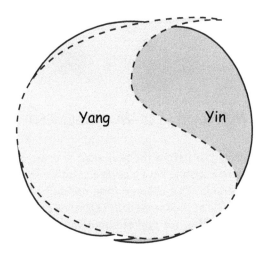

**Figure 3.2 Yang dominates Yin**

To us, the two qualities certainty and agreement have both a linear and mechanistic aspect to them. We show this here as a two-dimensional view of certainty and agreement (Figure 3.3). The horizontal axis represents a spectrum from 'close to certainty' to 'far from certainty'. Travelling along the vertical axis originates with 'close to agreement" until 'far from agreement' is reached. Any framework for thinking that bases itself on the 'close to' points of certainty and agreement, can only operate in what Mark Youngblood[17] calls 'calm water'. This is an environment characterized by certainty and predictability. We can see where he gets his imagery from when we think of a still pond. Imagine what happens when something is thrown in. The ripple caused by a stone thrown in the pond will fade away and the pond will return to its stillness (its' state of equilibrium). This can be predicted with some certainty and agreement, based on past observation of ponds.

---

[17] Youngblood, M. (1997) *Life at the Edge of Chaos: Creating the Quantum Organization*, Richardson, Texas, Perceval Publishing.

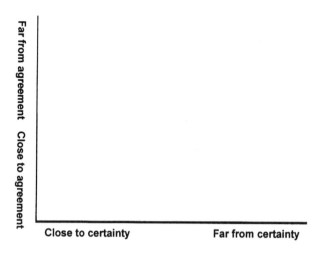

**Figure 3.3 Certainty and Agreement Axis**

No doubt you will have heard about the charge that organizations try to run themselves 'like clockwork'. Where did this come from? Youngblood[18] (p41) joins many management writers when he talks about Newton, the physicist who:

> '...articulated an entirely new, mechanistic view of the universe that ultimately overthrew the nature-centered, holistic outlook that had prevailed for more than a millennia... The prevailing mindset of dominance, control, and separateness provided the cornerstone of their ideas... Newton's ghost haunts the corridors and boardrooms of our corporations ...'

Now we would like to link the ideas of the Newtonian mechanistic view of the world and apply it to management and see what happens. Is there a place for mechanistic management? We would say that there will always be a place for routines and mechanizing. The difference in our thinking is that we envisage organizations not as machines but organizations who enfold machine-like elements into holistic and organic mindsets. Some of the components in the mechanistic mindset

---

[18] Youngblood, M. (1997) *Life at the Edge of Chaos: Creating the Quantum Organization.* Richardson, Texas, Perceval.

will be very familiar to most of us. At the top of the list are the rules, regulations and procedures that have become the centre-piece for many organizations. In the vernacular, sometimes rules and regulations become the tail that wags the organizational dog.

Mechanistic Management describes the zone where people within the organization share a common paradigm or mental model. (A paradigm is a set of learned views or the lens through which we view the world. It is a set of beliefs that we have about the world, its boundaries and how problems are solved within those boundaries). Here people are in agreement as to how the organization operates or should operate. Feedback loops operate in an affirming way so that the shared paradigm is never questioned, nor are the beliefs and values that underpin the paradigm.

In mechanistic management, these values are about conformity and convergence. Decisions are made using technically rational processes because there is agreement about the environment in which the organization operates, and how the organization should be run. Also, control is practiced in hierarchical or bureaucratic forms. All of these are practiced to ensure predictability and harmony.

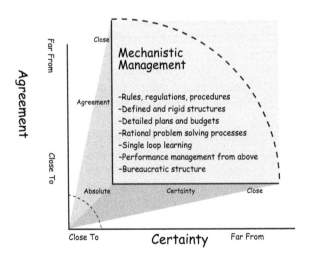

**Figure 3.4 Mechanistic Management**

Some of the features of Mechanistic Management are captured in Figure 3.4. Adherence to the values of close to certainty and close to agreement (rules and regulations embody these values) mean that instead of moving, as circumstances require, into uncertainty and disagreement, the mechanistic image is projected so that the prevailing paradigmatic needs can be met. In other words, there is no progression as things change and become volatile. Instead, volatility is met with the same systemic response of rules and regulations that work in 'calm water' environments.

## Rules, Regulations and Procedures

The first thing we want to say here is that rules have a long history. Underlying rules, regulations and procedures is a set of assumptions. It was (and is) assumed that rules bring about social order. They seek to regulate behaviour and overcome personal choice. They rely on a view of the world where everything is factual. Not only that, but facts are part of logic and rational thinking. There is a moral authority to rules, imparted by those who make them, that people 'ought' to behave in a compliant way.

Because of these assumptions, rules, regulations and procedures are not set up to be challenged, to have the certain transformed to the uncertain, and to brook any disagreement. In other words, when we act within the 'legal face' of the organization, we operate in close to certainty and close to agreement conditions. Here we learn to govern our organizations through the application of fairly rigid rules, regulations and procedures. This makes sense when we live in an environment of certainty and agreement. These conditions, for most of us, are all we have ever known in our management existence. We would like to propose here that there is a 'sometimes yes and sometimes no' to the idea of rules, regulations and procedures always prevailing.

Let's look at some examples. Safety procedures such as the isolation of equipment are necessary. Similarly, product specifications are essential. Ingredients, recipes or elements to make a standardised product are necessary. These have fixed variables that if adhered to will produce a predicted outcome. The rules, regulations and procedures in these examples were developed from past experience. Only if there is a reasonable assurance that today will look like yesterday will these continue to be appropriate. If yesterday's safety environment changes, products change, materials change and so on then it would not make sense to apply yesterday's rules to today's needs.

In almost every aspect of business, paradoxes occur. In the case of rules and regulations, the hope is that paradox does not occur. In fact the more rules-based an organization is, the less likely it is to embrace the notion of paradox. We suggest that yes; there will always be a need for rules, regulations and procedures. Yet just as surely, there will be a need for spontaneity and self-organizing, as situations that are new and uncertain emerge.

On the certainty side, organizations are subject to legislative rules and regulations. They seek to deliver the certainty and predictability sought by most societies. To have a *license to operate* or permission to exist, organizations must be prepared to meet the external demands placed upon them. There is no choice - laws and regulations must be complied with. Also, most people require boundaries within which they can operate. To not have boundaries may lead to confusion in areas where some certainty is needed. Once again, our conversation leads us into paradox.

How can rules, regulations and procedures operate in both stable and changing ways? How can they become living responsive documents, as they need to be? How can they be de-coupled from a reliance on the past? To us, the answer lies in an assumption that employees and managers together are architects of the present and the future. Alongside the 'product' of rules, the process of constant review and 'fit' needs to happen, and in a participative way.

**Questions to ponder**

In what area of your organization are rules, regulations and procedures necessary? (Think variables)
Does the organization revise these rules, regulations and procedures as the variables in the environment change?
If not, why do you think this is?

## Defined and Rigid Structures

Managers will often find that there is a reliance on formal and defined structures to manage the relationships between functions and the people within those functions. When these are rigidly defined, the system requires a context of certainty, where there is general agreement as to how it should operate.

Structure and its companion, restructuring activities, are usually the result of past experiences and it is only in the past that certainty and agreement exists. What if the organization's present structure limits future possibility? Many organizations hire or promote people for their specialist knowledge or expertise. Do you think that this would encourage or discourage the free sharing of information and expertise? Sharing might happen but this would almost be in spite of the structure.

It is interesting to observe how frequently organizations make structural changes in response to poor performance. Since this generally does not achieve the desired result (of improving performance), it suggests that the wrong tool (restructuring) is being used. The restructuring strategy is doomed to fail where the assumption is of a world that is stable and one in which agreement exists. This is an assumption that is clearly invalid. We only need to look around at technology, globalization, and multiple customers in multiple markets to check the invalidity of the assumption of stability and predictability.

It seems apparent that even if something does not work, human beings keep doing it. How many times have you heard a parent say to a child, 'If I have told you once, I have told you a thousand times….?' I wonder what makes us think that it will work on the 1001st occasion. How many times do we need to restructure before we realise that this strategy is of limited use?

Rigid structures are tools that are used to limit behaviour. They clearly define the boundaries of the work available to an individual and the authority of each individual to make decisions. Rigid structures are used to maintain control and co-ordination in the level above (which is why we often feel shackled by bureaucracy). This, in turn, is supposed to ensure certainty, predictability and stability. Restructuring is most useful where the organization is in a stable and predictable environment and where it is not overly concerned with messy human behaviour.

Putting the activity of restructuring in a different frame, a complexity frame, there is no doubt from listening to employees that equilibrium, or steady state, is disturbed when restructuring happens. However, if the management objective is to move away from equilibrium by causing structural disturbance, restructuring can be used to generate tension within the organization, which in turn generates energy. A key issue here though is whether the organization has the supporting systems in place to avail itself of opportunities.

**Question to ponder**

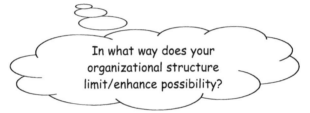

In what way does your organizational structure limit/enhance possibility?

**Detailed Plans and Budgets**

The area of mechanistic management is where we find a passion for detailed plans and budgets. To create detailed budgets and plans assumes certainty is possible. A basic human desire for security is expressed through our need for detailed plans and budgets. Unfortunately, in real life, there are very few situations where our ability to plan and predict is sophisticated enough to enable the expectations of those budgets to be achieved. Perhaps, this is why many of us find the budget process a difficult exercise on which to enthusiastically apply our energy. We know intuitively that the detailed budget is a fantasy, but we are required to play the political game to ensure our personal survival.

If certainty existed in the market place it would not be possible to profit from buying and selling shares on the stock exchange. If everyone was able to predict movements in share prices, (that is, there was certainty and agreement among the participants) then everyone would make the same buying and selling decisions and profits could not be achieved from trading activities.

Perhaps in other areas of endeavour, certainty and agreement is achievable. If for example, you were producing packaging for well established, common breakfast cereals, detailed forecasting and budgeting may be possible since the type of packaging does not change significantly over time and the sales are predictable through the application of statistical techniques.

From the above two examples we can see that the common factor determining predictability (or not) is variation (certain or uncertain). Neither is right or wrong. Simply put, the nature of the variables is different. Some are known and some are unknown. This is where we need to take note. Any person with knowledge of statistical analysis knows that to predict with certainty, one must know the variables and their behaviour, and also, be able to control them – a fundamental Newtonian exercise.

**Question to ponder**

Have you ever experienced a plan or budget not working out as planned? Why was this? Can you identify the variables and their behaviour and why and how this affected your plans?

**Rational Problem Solving Processes**

Another feature of mechanistic management is the passion for rational problem solving processes. Rational processes rely on concrete facts and data to achieve certainty and secure agreement. They are the tools of control when certainty and agreement are possible.

All problems have a set of variables, that is things or activities whose behaviour or properties are subject to variation. Decisions about how variables might interact within a given set of circumstances give the problem-solver some alternatives from which to choose. The issue then becomes choosing the alternative that will give most benefit. Of great benefit to rational problem solvers is an accurate knowledge of the behaviour of all variables. Cause and effect reasoning can then provide links that allow forecasting of the consequences of each of the alternative solutions

The objective in rational problem solving is to reduce ambiguity until opportunities are clear. The questions to be asked can be specific and any difficulties that exist lie in finding the answers to specific questions. Disagreements are settled by rational debate, the exercise of hierarchical power, or through negotiation and political bargaining. We have all experienced the problem solving sessions where we know that some one (higher up) has decided what to do before the solution is offered. Where the activity is technical rather than political, where variables are clear, (e.g. operation of machinery) problems can be solved with some degree of certainty. This, in turn allows people to operate close to agreement with one another.

Again, in an environment that is close to certainty and agreement, rational processes are legitimate tools to use. It is useful to stress here that we are talking about the application of rational processes to situations *where there is limited variation*. We strongly support the application of rational processes to the physical or business processes of the organization. In fact, we argue strongly that it is essential for physical and legal business processes to be managed with certainty and with absolute agreement. Later in the chapter we call this a *license to operate*.

However, it has been perplexing and disappointing for us to observe many organizations who inappropriately apply rational problem solving processes to 'human systems' where there is infinite variability and unpredictability. In this type of environment, a rational linear problem-solving process is therefore of very limited use if useful at all. What works for machinery only applies to human beings when they are seen as extensions to machinery. The assumption that simple linear relationships exist between people – a clear example of the application of Newtonian thinking – underestimates the overlay of values, moods, judgements and intuitions that individuals bring to the workplace.

We suggest when we are working with clients and customers, that a core element in achieving high levels of performance is the development of technical competency. People need to feel secure in their job skills and technical knowledge before they will embrace the social competencies required for more-than-ordinary, or extraordinary performance. No one in his or her right mind would want to see a production or business process exhibiting uncontrolled variation. Hofstede[19] describes this as 'Routine Control', where there is no ambiguity about the targets to be achieved and performance is accurately measured, with the cause-effect link clearly understood and predictable. This system generates *a negative (intentionally limiting) feedback loop* that tells the observer of the deviation from the target and often feeds back the information automatically into the process.

Hofstede's other type of control that seems to fit in to the area of mechanistic management, is called *expert control*. This he describes as very close to routine control but without the requirement that the activities are repetitive and allowing for some expert intervention to occur. Here the actual outcomes are reported against projections and people decide what to do to remove the variances.

**Question to ponder**

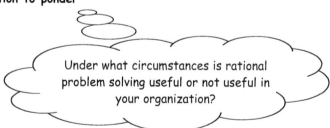

Under what circumstances is rational problem solving useful or not useful in your organization?

**Single Loop Learning**

Learning is the heartbeat of many organizations. Within the mechanistic management framework, just as in the extraordinary leadership framework there are many opportunities for learning.

---

[19] Hofstede, G. (1981) *Management Control of Public and Non-profit Activities.* Accounting, Organizations & Society, Vol 6, No 3.

We will describe single loop learning which is highly achievable in mechanistic management.

Single loop learning is where a problem or a fault is taken at face value and solved. Say a light bulb blows three times in a week. The single loop learner will learn and have practice in how to change the light bulb, perhaps experimenting with screw in and lock-in types of connections.

As we see in chapter five where we talk about learning cultures, double loop learning is where the learner goes one level deeper in looking at the problem. What is causing the light bulb to blow?

Is the wiring faulty? Is the connection itself faulty? Is the circuit carrying too much power so that as soon as the light is required it breaks down? Here the focus is not on the light bulb but on the electricity system.

One of the features of mechanistic management is that it is specific and efficient. Note that in single loop learning the context was bounded by the immediate problem. It would be inefficient to broaden the brief to that of discovery. Historically also, some of the devices aimed to protect employees against possible exploitation, such as demarcation of tasks and trades, not only aided single loop learning but it made any other sort virtually impossible to achieve. From double to triple loop learning the enterprise is less certain. The learning conversation has been broadened and sometimes the learning outcome ends up asking more questions than it can supply answers.

Once this stage has been reached, the activity resembles that of creativity and innovation. Where these two qualities are desired, the organization needs to free up the parameters it uses to monitor and assess learning. In single loop learning the parameter is around the light bulb problem. The assessment concerns 'does the light now work'? In triple loop learning the parameter is much wider and more uncertain. The assessment needs to be more on improving learning processes than on immediate outcomes. The point we have made earlier about limiting the thinking is very germane here. Organizations that want or need to be creative and innovative put systemic barriers in the way if they design structures and systems of the 'does it work now?' variety.

## Performance Management from Above

Performance management within a hierarchical and mechanistic environment continues the theme of the search for certainty. It is uni-dimensional, directing behaviour towards a reachable end (goal or target). The worst-case scenario is when the boss takes sole responsibility for establishing and monitoring the targets to be achieved in the next accounting period. Those actions assume that this is done in an environment of certainty and agreement. Such a stance demands submission to the authority of the boss. This tells people that the boss knows best – that a fundamental and most trustworthy source of knowledge exists beyond oneself.

It seems obvious that such a top-down relationship can only exist when we are in a position that is close to certainty and agreement. The boss has to feel confident that he or she can predict with a high level of certainty, what is going to happen during the forthcoming accounting period. In reality, this ability to predict is rare because of the uncertainty of the world in which our organizations live. Also, the very thing that makes individuals valuable, their ability to think, to judge, to relate and to self-organize prevents prediction.

**A scenario to ponder - How does a top-down type of relationship limit opportunities?**

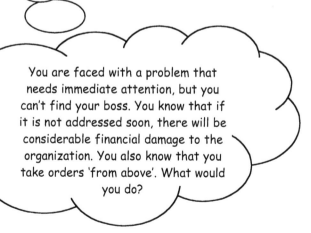

You are faced with a problem that needs immediate attention, but you can't find your boss. You know that if it is not addressed soon, there will be considerable financial damage to the organization. You also know that you take orders 'from above'. What would you do?

### The Bureaucratic Structure

The bureaucratic structure that we talked about earlier is a cornerstone feature of mechanistic management. The very design of levels above and levels below intimates stability and even permanence. In fact one of the reasons that change seems to go against the grain in some organizations is that it is in contrast with this stable and enduring thing called bureaucracy. Bureaucratic structures are devoted to achieving and maintaining stability, certainty and predictability which we feature inside of the arc of mechanistic management (see Figure 3.4).

It could also be said that the idea that one can control for certainty puts people under considerable stress. They are being asked to do things and behave in ways that they know intuitively will not deliver organizational performance and survival – but because of the structure they can do nothing about it. This puts them in danger of developing a psychological state of 'learned helplessness'[20]. Experimental evidence supports that learned helplessness affects the immune and nervous system and can be a contributor to depression[21]. None of these conditions would be considered a factor leading to increased performance.

Further to this, such states can lead to victim mentality. Victim thinking is where a person believes that the things that happen to them are outside his or her control and usually in the control of others more powerful in the system. Over the years, people end up colluding with the 'I will control and you will be controlled' ethic that may cause them to feel trapped and become victims of the system in which they collude in maintaining – often there is no other choice for them and they feel helpless. The assumption of certainty in a patently uncertain world puts control assumptions in the realm of the unreal. To us and many others we know the one thing that is certain is that we live in a world of uncertainty.

---

[20] Maier S.F. & Seligman, M.E. P. (1976), *Learned Helplessness: Theory and Evidence.* Journal of Experimental Psychology: General. 105, 3-46. Seligman, M.E.P. (1993) *Learned Optimism.* Sydney, Random House Australia Pty Ltd.

[21] Laudenslager, M.L., Ryan, S.M., Drugan, R.C., Hyson, R.I. & Maier, S.P. (1983) *Coping and Immunosupression: Inescapable but not escapable shock suppresses lymphocyte proliferation.* Science, 221, 568-570. Visintainer, M.A., Volpicelli, J.R. & Seligman, M.E.P. (1982) *Tumor rejection in rats after inescapable or escapable shock.* Science, 216, 437-439.

In fact, part of the fantasy is that people actually believe that they can operate efficiently and effectively in a system that limits information, behaviour and opportunities. Bureaucratic structures usually restrict the information flows both coming in to the organization and within it. There is no need to have a constant flow of information because we see ourselves living in a world of certainty and agreement – so yesterday's information is sufficient for efficient and effective operation of the organization. Paradoxically, people know that survival can only occur when they are able to exercise flexible and adaptable behaviours, supported by rapid and open information flows.

**A scenario to ponder**

You have a great idea on how to increase performance/sales/production in your organization.

You want to share it with your boss, but you know that he is not open to suggestions. When you do summon the courage to approach him, he is controlling and arrogant, and says, 'I'm the boss, I'll tell you what to do and when'.

How would you feel? If another opportunity came your way would you share it with your boss again?

## The Attributes of Mechanistic Management

### i) License to Operate

It is here that we stress the importance of some of the mechanistic management activities that are essential to the survival of the organization. The external world requires that organizations have mechanistic management practices in place. Government regulators are responsible for the administration of industrial laws, environmental laws, taxation, trade practices, occupational health and safety. Compliance with the laws, rules and regulations is not an option, it is a demand. Failure to meet the demand could result in an organization suffering severe penalties.

The thing to remember though, is that compliance does not guarantee achieving potential. In fact, the two need to be seen as their distinct selves. Compliance is about limitation (intentional). Potential is about amplifying possibilities and achievement, often in a way that expands rather than limits. Transformational performance is the pursuit of the organization's true potential. It is counter productive to limit potential. (see Figure 3.5)

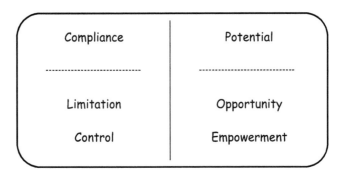

**Figure 3.5 Compliance vs Potential**

Speaking of potential, or transformational performance, we think of things that we had not thought of, or not thought of in a creative way. This leads us to think of areas or zones of thinking. First there is the zone of things we know, of which we are fairly 'certain' and we call this 'close to certainty'. Then there is that creative space where we shoot the breeze using our other, sometimes underused, capabilities. These would include thinking with our intuition, our imagination, our fun side. Some colleagues call this 'white water' thinking as opposed to the 'calm water' thinking of compliance. This sort of thinking takes us 'far from certainty'. It is only in this area that organizational transformation occurs.

Now, if we understand that the nature of Mechanistic Management is to control and limit <u>intentionally</u>, how can we at the same time help the organization to grow to reach its' full potential, also considering the unpredictable world in which we live? First, we suggest identifying what we can and can't control or limit, so we can understand what type of management or leadership to use, where, with what and when – we call this 'judgement'.

## ii) Control and Limitation

The simplest way of identifying what is appropriate to control or limit is to look at the variables involved. For starters, ask 'are they all known, or are some unknown?' For example, let's look at the business accounting system – do we know our turnover, our expenditure, our assets and so on? Yes – our variables are known and we can safely say that this exercise lies in the area of certainty and agreement.

In some cases, however, regarding forecasting there may be variability that we can't successfully predict – just when we think we're back on the rails, something unpredictable happens (been there?).

Let's take for example forecasting production rates when production is dependent on tight supply schedules. What are the variables here? Are there some variables that we have no control over e.g. ships, weather, strikes and so on? Could something happen that is beyond our present knowledge? We don't know all the variables or their behaviours, so how can we forecast accurately? To add to this, we have the complexity of human nature. Organizations are human systems, and you would know being one yourself, that sometimes, humans vary their perceptions, their beliefs, their needs, their promises, their emotions, and their behaviour from day to day. Imposing limits would not be sensible as complexity and uncertainty increases.

So first, we need to understand the nature of human beings and the world in which we live. Individual characteristics are infinitely variable and impossible to control. 'Reality' is what people interpret it to be. They apply their values and beliefs sometimes (such as in terrorist examples) with devastating consequences. Even so, there is no denying the richness and variety of thinking available to us in organizations. We need to ask ourselves the question.... 'Do we want to amplify or limit the organization's potential?' If we based our answer on the easiest option, we might opt to limit. If we based our answer on opportunity for growth, both personal and organizational, then we would want to amplify potential-giving opportunities. The reason is that by limiting potential and growth, we would be, in our view, setting the organization up for failure.

Yet we still seem to support systems (dependent on known and predictable variables) that set us up to fail. Why is this? Think of a competitive football team. It does not matter how many times the team watches the other teams in action, there is nothing but uncertainty on the day. Imagine being coached to check with various team members and the captain for permission to pass the ball. By the time it was granted the opposing team would be laughing all the way to the goalpost. Yes, both teams have an element of certainty in the rules of the game. Within this parameter, though, the individual plays and cross plays very quickly make the rules the only constant in the game. The rest is uncertain and unpredictable.

Now let's compare a football match to the world in which we live. In basic terms, instead of variables that don't change, (and change has accelerated in the last fifty years since World War II) we are now working with variables that do change from one week to the next. In fact, they change from moment to moment and sometimes we don't even know what they are until they're upon us. We are back to the paradox again. Mechanistic Management (systems, strategies, and processes) relies on variables that don't change. We need some of these to have a *license to operate* and to ensure that where variables are known and stability is present, the appropriate approach is selected. However, the other, increasingly visible face of business life is permeated with uncertainty. There is lack of agreement as to what is happening and how best to resolve issues, volatility in almost every aspect of the environment and increasing pressures to innovate and create. We have drawn on some of the writers referred to so far in the book (Stacey, Wheatley, Youngblood) for our inspiration in presenting to you our framework for combining the certain with the uncertain through the use of what we call the transformational edge.

**Questions to ponder**

What areas of your organization would best run by Mechanistic Management?

In what areas of your organization is Mechanistic Management
a)   Suitable?
b)   Not suitable?

# Notes

# TRANSFORMATIONAL EDGE

We begin this chapter by setting the scene for the transformational edge. The theory of complex adaptive systems well portrayed by Youngblood[22] contributed to our thinking alongside the broader complexity theory that led us to our various endeavours in management activities. An important contribution for this book is, of course, David's Extraordinary Leadership Program. At least five thousand people have experienced this program and is an example of both constant adaptation and 'at the edge' thinking.

### Complex Adaptive Systems

In complex adaptive systems (CAS) we accept that many of the elements and variables in a situation may not be known, or not fully known. Furthermore, we accept that the impact is far-reaching and complex. A key to thinking about complex adaptive systems is thinking about natural order coming out of chaos. Alternatively you can think of the islands of order that exist even in the most chaotic systems. Think of a heated argument that is compounded by people coming in and going out of the room and chipping in anyway. (We are thinking now about an actual conversation during one of the team meetings in the Extraordinary Leadership Program that we bring you later.) You are seeing a complex adaptive system at work. The talk is going round and round. At the same time three mini-conversations are going on with the speakers coming in to the main one when the left ear hears something that merits comment. There is over-talking, laughter, cynicism and these all interact comfortably. At times, something draws immediate and concentrated attention and the level of noise and interest increases. The feedback loops in the conversation fasten on something and it is amplified. Other elements of the conversational loops dampen

---

[22] Youngblood, M. (1997) *Life at the Edge of Chaos: Creating the Quantum Organization*, Richardson, Texas, Perceval Publishing.

down. When we say non-linear, this is what we mean. Its' opposite is what we call the mutual monologue. Each person is speaking at his or her turn. As one finishes, the other begins. We sometimes call this the 1+1 = 1 conversation as each person is having one conversation and the sum also equals one conversation. On the other hand, the complex adaptive system is open to everything and everything is open to the system. It is not orderly and yet somehow, some sort of order is naturally produced. In the complex adaptive system people are adapting to others who are also adapting to others and so on. Impossible, you say? Look at our neural networks that allow us to think, feel, judge, avoid pain and danger and, simultaneously, appreciate music, our friends, and the beauty of a rainbow. Most of us can think casually, plan the day, consider a friend's problem, wash the car and smile at a half – forgotten joke all in a disjointed but satisfying way.

The same applies in organizations if we let it. As in nature, even when things look chaotic, (and that is also a term, often associated with uncertainty and complexity) patterns do emerge. Take the all-important management and well-loved activity of strategic planning. It is interesting to observe that people seem to be obsessed with strategic management as an orderly and conformist process with certainty and predictability a fundamental aim. Patterns are what strategy is about if we let them emerge. They emerge in real life of course, because in practice and for survival we find people continually adjusting their strategies to the ever-changing circumstances presented by interacting feedback loops and incoming information. The interesting conclusion is that when people work together in organizations their behaviour impacts on others in unique and continually changing ways. Their interactions are non-linear in nature. They construct meaning as they go and this meaning always adds a layer of complexity to situations. This makes life full of surprises as people reinterpret things and act upon them to make them their own. In this way, through owning things, individuals and groups in the organization determine the way 'things are actually done'.

In presenting the transformational edge, we hope to inspire managers. It is the expectations they have been conditioned to hold that keep them in the linear and simple loop. They are expected to make the organization predictable and stable by putting rules and systems in place. Of course, logically speaking, once these were in place we would have no further need for managers. In real life, managers are needed because the rules do not fit unique and changing circumstances. Managers are needed to change, bend or reinterpret the rules to ensure that the organization operates.

We propose that the 'better' the organization is at conditioning managers to stay in the traditional (what we call mechanistic) mode, the more likely managers are likely to seek 'certain' information (the facts) and to reject the tacit, intuitive information that is less certain but more creative. We launch to the topic of the transformational edge with an idea from a critical writer on institutionalism and human adaptation.

Human beings are culture building creatures. People have creative capabilities and represent a step beyond the organic or biological adaptation to the stresses of the environment in the direction of intellectual adaptation. Intellect and the human capacity for speech, the creation of language and the creation of tools have allowed for selective and purposeful adaptation. People will adapt according to their own ideas, conceptualizations and values.

In other words, it is futile to try to pin people down as passive recipients of rules and regulations, even when these are clear and reasonable. We need to assume that people de-construct and re-construct reality as they talk to each other and make sense of things. People knock ideas around and play with them, even when they are more irrational than rational. They do this naturally and it is this element of natural activity that zigzags between the real and the imagined that we present in the concept of the transformational edge.

What is interesting about the transformational edge is that it is located far from certainty and far from agreement. What do we mean by the transformational edge? It is a metaphorical boundary for thinking. Over this boundary, in conditions of uncertainty, transformational thinking takes place. When you step into the transformational zone you have entered the world of unknowns, but you also enter the world of potentials. Here is where your imagination is given full reign, unimpeded (at this point) by operational 'will it work?' considerations. (Figure 4.1)

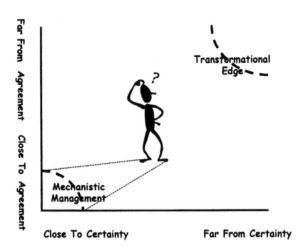

**Figure 4.1 Transformational Edge**

What we are utilizing here is the untapped resource of creative and innovative thinking that has little place in the prediction and control environment. In the transformational framework, the outcome is always some sort of innovation because it evolves out of thinking about potentials, not certainties. Of course, once certainty has been left behind, the situation becomes more precarious for the thinker. The sense of balance, of equilibrium or homeostasis is disturbed. Tension is produced. But this can be quite motivating as we see in the psychological *drive model of motivation*[23]. As needs or tension increases, motivation increases. This is driven by homeostasis, 'the management of a balanced or constant internal state'. When we are close to certainty and close to agreement often we are not 'pressed' to be innovative – there is no *need*. However, when at the 'edge', tension increases along with the need for homeostasis. This is when motivation increases, leading us to think of new ways, or adjustments to existing ones, as Myers[24] suggests '...*systems operate through feedback loops, with adjustments based on information continually fed back into the system*'. When transformational thinking has produced insights and innovation it is time to deliver what we call 'order in chaos' by uniting the certain and the uncertain.

---

[23]Myers, D.G. (1992) *Psychology*. New York, Worth, (p353).
[24]Ibid

A paradox you may think and you would be right. We are proposing a shift from 'either/or' thinking to 'both/and' thinking. We owe a debt to the writers on chaos, represented by James Gleick[25] and Ilya Prigogine[26]. We are using metaphors from chaos and complexity theory to present some of our ideas about where order (or chaos) fit into the scheme of things. Take our idea of the transformational edge. Here the organizational system is said to be working at the *edge of chaos*, which is where new forms of thinking emerge. The idea of chaos conjures up for many people thoughts of disintegration and organizational 'death'. Chaos does not equal disintegration of the system. Chaos contains order without predictability. Behaviour is not stable, nor is it totally bounded. Creativity sits well here, characterized as it is by the discovery of the unknown and invention. In chaos theory, the edge is not a precise point – it is not like a cliff that you can fall off.

Chaos begins where certain knowledge and linear thinking end. The certain is replaced by the potential and the linear is replaced by the non-linear. There is a strong adaptive character to transformational thinking. It is when interactions in a non-linear system occur that things become unpredictable. Chaos is created by information feeding back on itself and changing or transforming in the process. Another way to put this is to say that 'more goes out than comes in'. We have all been in situations like the one described next where what seems like a relatively small disturbance is fed into organizational processes. In Figure 4.2 we see a relatively small disturbance, 'd' going in to the system. Applying linear thinking will tell the manager that the disturbance will remain proportional to its input.

However, we see that there is an amplifier at work 'A'. As the disturbance goes around the feedback loops of non-linear thinking people are talking about the disturbance. As they talk they may make more judgements. If these are negative, it is possible that the disturbance gets bigger. We can hear the manager in whose area the disturbance began protesting that 'this is ridiculous – it has been blown up out of all proportion'. This was, of course to be expected had

[25] Gleick, J. (1998) *Chaos. The amazing science of the unpredictable*. London, Vintage.
[26] Prigogine, I (1996) *The End of Certainty*. New York, The Free Press.

the manager been attuned to non-linear thinking and therefore on the alert for amplifiers (such as opinion leaders) who might join the feedback loops. As we say below, the act of amplifying the disturbance has a way of changing it.

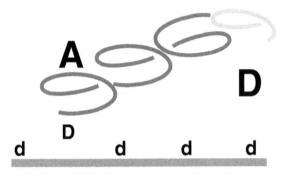

**Figure 4.2 Feedback and Amplifier**

Gleick[27] has provided many illustrations of non-linear relationships. Let's take friction for example.

> *Without friction a simple linear equation expresses the amount of energy you need to accelerate a hockey puck. With friction the relationship gets complicated, because the amount of energy changes depending on how fast the puck is already moving. Non-linearity means that the act of playing the game has a way of changing the rules. You cannot assign a constant importance to friction, because its importance depends on speed. Speed, in turn, depends on friction. That twisted changeability makes non-linearity hard to calculate, but it also creates rich kinds of behaviour that never occur in a linear system.*

On the other hand, linear relationships can be shown as a straight line. Problems can be solved and, systems can be taken apart and reassembled. In the case of non-linear systems, problems are not as simple, as solved parts cannot be reassembled in exactly the same way as they were. So are we saying that there are no boundaries in this sort of thinking? Amazingly, we are not and we owe to nature the

---

[27] Gleick, J. (1998) *Chaos. The Amazing Science of the Unpredictable.* London, Vintage, (p24).

discovery of a phenomenon that acts as a magnet, drawing behaviours inside a boundary but in a mysterious rather than prescribed way. The discovery by physicists of the 'strange attractor' seems to mimic what we ourselves have found in organizations that have strong governing principles and people committed to making them work.

**Strange Attractors**

Strange attractors exhibit a magnetic pull. You have all, we are sure, seen a person or an organization that 'has pull'. People are drawn in as though by a magnet. The concept, the drawing inside of some boundaries or ways of thinking is called a strange attractor. It is strange because no one can really explain it, any more than you can explain what draws you to one person and not another. Another example is how people draw together in the event of a disaster.

Once inside a strange attractor boundary (which is intangible and tacit) all the very different organizational inputs will stay inside as though there was a magnet drawing them in. And the interesting thing is that order comes out of so many differences. So far, we are well, if not over-trained in being kept inside of explicit and tangible boundaries by the rules, regulations and structures. We are not too well developed in trusting the human being's capacity to self organise and produce order from seeming chaos.

Of course people putting their own versions of organizing into a system is guaranteed to knock it out of its comfortable state of equilibrium. Yet, over and over again, we witness our capacity to produce new forms of order. Just look at a busy junction when the traffic lights don't work. Does the traffic come to a halt because the official regulators (traffic lights) don't work? Not at all. People deal with the complexity and are responsive to information coming in from all over the junction. Similarly, watch a busy uncontrolled pedestrian intersection – it seems chaotic, but somehow there is order as each person going in different directions arrives at the other side of the street.

What is often missed is the very sophisticated process that goes on when people are naturally dealing with complexity. As complexity increases, information is generated that triggers different responses. In many cases, the responses can have an amplified effect on what is happening, such as the one we described earlier. Even if initial changes are small, the result can be large because the information being fed back grows to the point where it cannot be ignored. At this point the system *in its current state* can fall apart. To those who need and seek order and certainty it means the death of the system *as it is*. This situation can lead to a re-invention of the organization *as it can be*. The system, once released from the shackles imposed by expectations of continuity and stability can reconfigure or transform itself into a higher form that can deal with changing environments.

Another metaphor for thinking about organizations is the fractal. The interesting and exciting quality of the fractal to us is the existence of 'initial conditions'. This is best explained by something from the physical world. An equilateral triangle takes its rules from the number and length of sides and where they are in relation to each other. We call these 'initial conditions'. A square is differentiated by its initial conditions. Even though sides are of equal length and meet at each apex, the square has an initial condition different from the triangle. Let us relate this to an organization. Metaphorically we can think of core values and governing principles as initial conditions. They have parameters that are unique to the organization. They determine the 'shape' of the organization and differentiate it from others. One of the most heard criticisms of values and principles in organizations is the use to which they are often put. The most common example is where the vision and mission are generated with great commitment and participation only to be framed, hung on the wall and forgotten. One sure way of obscuring values and principles is to have a forests of rules and procedures that seem to grow and take on a life of their own.

How does the concept of fractals help our thinking? Well the thing about fractals is that they retain their shape at whatever magnification you care to name. A tree has a fractal shape. Leaves, branches, and the overall tree, all reflect the shape. When you see the shape of the leaf you are seeing the shape of the tree itself. The tiniest part is a microcosm of the larger whole. Why is it that we are not confident that this can happen in organizational life? Why can we not look at a person, a team, a department and, in all cases, 'see' the organization? A side effect of the proliferation of rules, procedures, and structures that grow almost daily is that it soon becomes hard, if not impossible, to detect the core of the organization, its reason for being. Another way to say this is its initial conditions. We have represented this as triangles in Figure 4.3 which stand for core values and governing principles. Individuals and groups act in self-similar ways but as you can see here, there are different combinations and expressions. Structures, systems and procedures support (not control) in an adaptive way. Rules become guidelines and structures have the flexibility they need to constantly adapt.

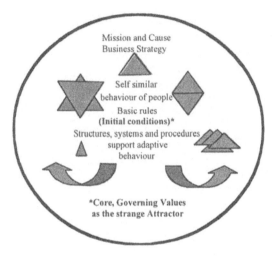

**Figure 4.3 Self-similarity and the strange attractor**

A second issue is that of disturbance. If managers do not like disturbance it is likely to be because it knocks the status quo out of balance. They see things 'falling apart' and their good work from the past destroyed. This is more a function of living in and valuing the past as a reference point for the future. Looking at it another way, the things that we fear most – disturbance and being out-of-balance – need not be signs of destruction, rather they are the source of creativity. Meg Wheatley writes in her book, *Leadership and the New Science*[28]:

---

[28] Wheatley, M. (1994 p20) *Leadership and the New Science: Learning about Organization from an Orderly Universe*. San Francisco, Berrett-Koehler.

*We have even found order in the event that epitomizes total disorder – chaos. Chaos theory has given us images of 'strange attractors' – computer pictures of swirling motion that traces the evolution of a system. A system is defined as chaotic when it becomes impossible to know where it will be next. There is no predictability; the system is never in the same place twice. But as chaos theory shows, if we look at such a system long enough and with the perspective of time, it always demonstrates its inherent orderliness. The most chaotic of systems never goes beyond certain boundaries; it stays contained within a shape that we can recognize as the system's strange attractor.*

Chaos – the word fills managers with dread. It is where we cease to understand the variables that govern our systems and processes. Look at nature. We live in natural systems (after all we, as humans are complex living systems) yet the prospect does not fill us with the same dread. We know that the weather is a chaotic system – the best scientists cannot predict it and in any case we would know better than to arrange outside events on the strength of their predictions. Allegiance to acting on predictions is what gives us the fear of chaotic systems in the workplace. Beyond the edge of chaos is where the system disintegrates or there is massive avoidance exercised by people.

Yes we are recommending, certainly to those organizations that believe in organizational renewal, the benefits of learning about and embracing chaos concepts. Why is this you might ask? Because we believe that it is at the transformational edge that new life and forms of existence are created. It is where our thinking results in innovation and creativity.

The implications for leadership at this point are both interesting and challenging. The core competency for an effective leader is the ability to embrace paradox and challenge simple linear thinking, accepting that at least part of the organization will display non-linear tendencies. Non-linearity can produce both amplifying and dampening feedback, it contains at the same time stability and instability – opposites that we do not find in the linear world of simple cause and effect.

At the transformational edge or the edge of chaos, the tools of mechanistic management are of little use. For example, what would happen if the football coach said 'we need to be adaptable and prepared for any situation that arises' – then when the team players use their initiative, he yells at them and tries to control them? Soon you would have a team that did not respond to the ever-changing challenges and became totally dependent on the leader. Similarly, the manager who is well versed in nurturing a compliant or even an obedience culture would struggle. The question becomes, therefore, if the known tools and experiences that we have had are of little use, what can we do?

Do we change the tools or do we change the tool bag? For us there is no contest. We would change the tool bag from a container for control-tools to one of self-organizing tools.

**Situation to ponder**

Peter has been living in the mechanistic zone for 27 years as a mechanical engineer in a production workshop. He's starting to learn about 'stepping out' beyond mechanistic management as he realises how limiting it is. In particular, he has been missing opportunities and not recognizing new and better ways of operating. He's actually going to the edge of transformation. But what does he do? How does he behave extraordinarily?

Develop this story by completing......
The first thing Peter would do is.....
Then he would...

# Notes

# EXTRAORDINARY LEADERSHIP

As we have been talking about managers up to now why, you may ask, have we suddenly changed to leaders? The reason was something of an insight for us. Managers who have to (or choose to) operate in the traditional, mechanistic mould really do manage. They see to it that people are in the right place at the right time with the right equipment. Additionally, they see that they are supported by once-removed leadership. This comes in the guise of rules, regulations, procedures and instructions. Learning is of the taught solutions variety and there is little necessity for everyone to be aware of the overall direction. What we are proposing in the extraordinary leadership model is that the very same managers we have just described can become leaders, champions of the organizational cause and facilitators of the organizational effort. In this chapter, we will present the same elements of management that we presented in chapter three but show how the thinking has changed to meet the requirements of extraordinary leadership.

As you can see at a glance (Figure 5.1), the extraordinary leader lives in a much richer and more complex world than his or her mechanistic counterpart. What lies between mechanistic management and the transformational edge is the subject of our interest. The extra dimensions result in extraordinary *leadership*. The tools needed to lead in situations of increasing uncertainty, and disagreement as to how to deal with that uncertainty, are a different set to those needed for mechanistic management.

Yet, we can hear you saying, there are situations where obedience and compliance to rules and regulations are needed. Yes, we agree. There are really no bad guys in our plot. Why not have both? Apply the more mechanistic methods when things are certain and people agree on what is what. Adopt transformational methods when (as is often the case these days) there is more turbulence than stability.

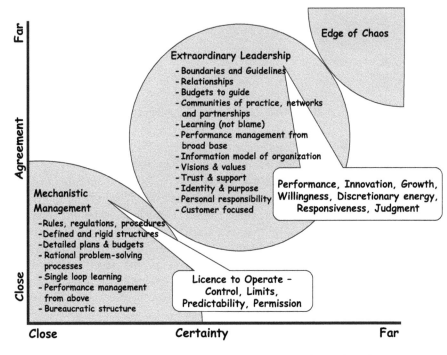

Copyright: David Napoli, 2004

**Figure 5.1 Extraordinary Leadership**

We talked earlier about mindsets and mental models. Another name for these is paradigms. As you can see by the following quotation from Stacey[29], old paradigms need to be 'shattered' before new ones such as we have been describing can be substituted. Stacey coined the term *extraordinary management*, defined below to capture this process.

> *Extraordinary management involves questioning and shattering paradigms, and then creating new ones. It is a process that depends critically upon contradiction and tension. Because it is outside the rules of an existing paradigm, because no one can know what new paradigms*

[29] Stacey, R.D. (1996) *Strategic Management & Organizational Dynamics 2nd Ed* London, Pitman. (p72)

*will be shared, because no one knows what the outcomes will be, rational analysis and argument cannot play much part in the developing of a new paradigm. Instead, frame-breaking extraordinary management is a process of persuasion and conversion, requiring contributions of champions. It is not about consistency or harmony, rather it is about destabilising and irregularity.*

We believe in the process of constant challenge, disintegration and renewal. In fact these qualities characterize us as people and also as a team of authors. This chapter captures our attempt to give to 'managers as leaders' a practical guide for leading in the circumstances of uncertainty and unpredictability that we talked about earlier. Like Stacey, especially considering the history of management theory and practices, to follow our guide would require extraordinary behaviour and thinking, the sort that managers would use in their leadership roles. Many of the ideas here have been tried and tested within organizations over a period of years.

So, what could extraordinary leaders be doing? We would like to invite you to our extraordinary leadership dance and take you on a journey into what the activities we outline in Figure 5.2 might look like. This list will be expanded in part two of chapter five.

## "EXTRAORDINARY" LEADERSHIP

## Performance = Direction + Willingness

- Boundaries and Guidelines
- Relationships
- Budgets to guide
- Communities of practice, networks and partnerships
- Learning (not blame)
- Performance management from broad base

Figure 5.2 Extraordinary Leadership In Action – Part 1

Our story begins with a mental equation. What were the foundations, we asked ourselves, on which extraordinary leaders needed to build? We bring you three central concepts, performance (by which we mean performing for potential), direction and willingness.

### Extraordinary Leadership: Performance = Direction + Willingness

It seems to us that within mechanistic management there is a sharp and somewhat exclusive focus on the *direction* that the managers of an organization wish to take. Rules, regulations, forecasts and budgets set the direction that is to be followed. Why not, you ask? Again, we meet our old friends 'limitation and control'. For extraordinary leadership the question is whether these concepts allow opportunities to infuse new or creative energy into the business. Direction, then, to us, does not mean a prescribed route to some predetermined and achievable outcome. One danger in this is that many managers operate with the belief that if they get the prescribed direction right, people will be willing to follow.

This belief is far from most of our experiences. We often ask groups with whom we are working to imagine that it was ten years ago. They are asked to list the ways in which the organization's performance could be improved. We then ask them to undertake the same task for today's organization and compare the lists. In most cases the lists are surprisingly similar. Yet it is often patently clear that something is sadly lacking in both. That is commitment. This suggests that for ten years people have known what needed to be done to improve the performance of their organization – that is the *direction*. What was missing was the *willingness* to do something about it.

On the other hand, the willingness or discretionary energy seems to emerge from the practice of extraordinary leadership. Extraordinary leadership is about growth, possibilities and innovation - not limitation. Within this kind of leadership, people become keen to deliver the discretionary energy that exists in all of us. It just seems so natural to become passionately committed to high levels of performance under these circumstances.

One tool in the extraordinary leader's tool bag is the recognition of non-linear thinking and feedback loops. Some of these features help the leader to penetrate the informal social space of the organization. Within this space, through conversations and interactions, the 'reality' conveyed by formal communication would be deconstructed and then reconstructed. The reconstructed reality would almost always be the one acted upon. In practical terms, as an example, it works this way. A new supervisor arrives and she is given a pep talk about keeping her team in order. After observing for about a week, she decides that the tea breaks are really out of hand. They can range from 15 minutes to 20 minutes and there seems to be no logic to them. At the next team-briefing she announces the new rule that tea breaks are to be kept to the union rule of 15 minutes per person. A small disturbance, you might think. What happens next is that the feedback loops go into action. People talk, mull over the rule and the context. They make judgements about what the rule really means and this is how amplification happens.

This amplification can be negative or positive. As the new rule (and the new supervisor) is conversed about, messages become. Let's say that the supervisor has a good reputation and locates the rule within a call to the team members to support the organization and do their bit for the business by taking a reasonable tea-break. She might be forgiven (being new) for not bringing the problem itself to the team for resolution and there might be a positive amplification of the original message. Alternatively, this might be seen as yet one more nail in the coffin of empowerment and the message may be amplified in a negative way, the 'new' message being a lot stronger than the original one. If limiting and dampening practices are being applied to situations that require innovation, negative things are magnified.

People have many ways of showing their mistrust or displeasure. These include not passing on valuable information, not being willing to share thoughts about solutions, and feeling too disheartened to contribute ideas. Even worse than that is the feeling that employees are not all that significant to the organization. No wonder we have seen so many examples of apathy at work, often accompanied by increased energy and enthusiasm for outside interests. Leaders who are attuned to non-linear thinking and amplification would be like organizational detectives. Knowing that trivial problems can escalate and bring a workplace to a standstill means that they are constantly gathering organizational data of the 'deep listening' type.

Here is another example of the impact of an individual's behaviour on a large system. In the mining industry, the drill and blast employees are responsible for blasting the area to be mined in the case of an open-cut mine. They are given a 'grid pattern' to follow to ensure the precise area is blasted and the resulting rock is suitably sized for crushing. Should an individual choose to drill outside the grid because it requires too much effort to precisely locate where to drill, then the rocks could be too large to be crushed and milled. The consequences are that the whole crushing, milling and processing operation becomes 'bogged' and production ceases. Here, one small action has been magnified with the effect of dampening performance for the whole operation. Should the same individual feel commitment and willingness to achieve for the operation, following the pattern and putting out the extra energy would be a natural way of expressing enthusiasm for the job.

In the chapter on mechanistic management, we talked about rules and structure. Here, we present the idea of boundaries and guidelines and, as you can see, there are some differences.

## Boundaries and Guidelines

When we are far from certainty some rules may be of little use. After all, the rules were developed from past experience and will only be useful if today is identical to yesterday. In fact, should today vary from yesterday, these rules may lead to dysfunctional behaviour and inappropriate responses by the organization to current issues.

There are also some rules that should be fixed over time, however, and should not change under any circumstances. They lie without doubt, close to certainty and agreement and form the boundaries of the organization. The legislation under which the organization operates is a key boundary and the rules that support those legislative obligations, must be followed. Specifically, the laws that relate to taxation, environmental parameters, industrial relations, employment, and corporate governance, are examples of boundary issues. This is support for mechanistic management.

Other boundary issues include customers' and stakeholders' specifications, legislation, the organization's cardinal safety rules, budgets, the shared values of the organization, and a limited number of organization rules. Let us say a little about each of these.

Customer and stakeholder specifications become a boundary issue for the organization since those in the organization do not set them nor do they have the capacity to unilaterally change those specifications. Similarly, the legislation governing the employment of people and the management of industrial relations is outside the control of organizations, other than those that create and manage those pieces of legislation. And even in those cases, those organizations are bound by the existing regulations that support the legislation.

The idea that budgets form a boundary issue may seem interesting to many. Budgets, once agreed, become fixed unless they happen to be renegotiated and changed to meet unexpected situations. The important point here is that they are fixed at a particular point in time and constitute a boundary issue.

Shared (or agreed) values govern our behaviour in all circumstances. Therefore, they are an essential piece of stability when the organization is far from certainty and far from agreement and guide us on how to deal with each particular situation.

Whilst many things that govern the organization and its environment may change, the agreed values on all levels remain a constant. Without this being so, the organization would disintegrate through dysfunctional and political behaviour which has a negative outcome.

Whilst boundary issues tend to be fixed, many other organizational rules need to be approached with flexibility. These organizational rules need to be seen as guidelines that can be applied in 'normal' situations (i.e. close to certainty). However, personal judgement needs to be applied to their application as we move to a position that is far from certainty and far from agreement. Facing uncertainty and being far from agreement leaves us no choice but to seek *guidelines* more than rely on the rules of the past. Guidelines, like values, enable us to develop flexible responses to the issues that we are suddenly confronted with.

Perhaps the relationships talked about in the above text can be illustrated by Figure 5.3. Let us look at the military as an example. The military in peacetime relies very heavily on rules and regulations since it lives in a world that is close to certainty and agreement.

However, if we observe the operation of those special units such as the Special Air Services Regiment (SAS) within the Australian Army, we find that they also operate on values and guidelines when the regiment is in military action. This is because the environment in which the SAS operates is far from certain. In fact, often it is at the edge of chaos or beyond.

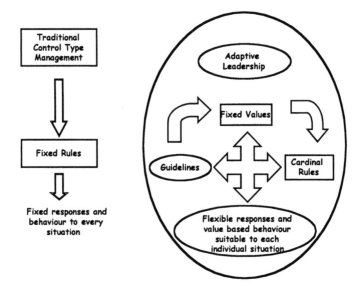

**Figure 5.3 Rules vs Values and Guidelines**

The opposing forces do not have rules nor do they operate by the established conventions of warfare. This results in the SAS needing to be flexible and responsive, in a way that adherence to rules does not permit. They do have a small number of rules that they honour because they are seen to be essential to safety and survival. Here we see the essence of jazz again. The underlying theme, those inviolable rules, those initial conditions and the improvisations from individuals all contribute to the theme in very different ways.

In the industrial environment, a small number of rules are adhered to under all circumstances. For example, in an industrial disaster, people will not violate the cardinal safety rule that forbids them to work on electrical equipment that has not been isolated. To do otherwise, has a high probability of death as its consequence.

In summary, we attempt to minimise rules and maximise guidelines when seeking high performance from our organizations. What becomes immediately apparent to us is that where we could rely on structures, as we describe in chapter three, we now need to rely on relationships.

## Relationships

Because of the importance of the individual in systems that are driven by non-linear feedback loops, relationships (not necessarily friendships) are of strategic importance.

You will have noticed that it is only relatively recently that relationships have been on the agenda for things like management development. Yet as writers like Dyer and Chu[30] found, they can have a double benefit of reducing costs and improving performance. We are not sure, even today, how many organizations think that the topic of relationship is not important enough to have on the training and development agenda. Yet we all know that relating to others successfully is of vital importance in working life. In 'ordinary', manager-directed relationships familiar to us, we find a mix of the written word, spasmodic mateship and an implicit yet strong boundary produced by 'manager-speak'. To lead in an extraordinary way requires us to develop strong and robust relationships as the fundamental core of leadership. Why? Because if we are not able to rely on rules, regulations and procedures to hold the system together and perform, we must rely on the relationships that we develop. To rely on relationships gives flexibility within the system to respond to uncertainty and unplanned events that a reliance on rules does not permit.

We will use the famous 'silos' as an example. Hierarchies and departmental boundaries encourage silos, or self-contained units that typically have a 'closed door' policy between departments. On one side of the door is 'them' and on the other side is 'us'. Constraining both 'them and us', of course, are the levels above.

---

[30] Dyer, J. H. and W. Chu (2003) The Role of Trustworthiness in Reducing Transaction Costs and Improving Performance: Empirical Evidence from the United States, Japan and Korea Organization Science 14(1), 57-68.

Silos by definition impede responsiveness and change in an organization. When we think of customers' needs constantly changing, as they do, then silos become sub-optimal by design. What happens if last minute changes need to be made during the process before a product is about to go on line in another department? Well it is not too difficult to guess. What may save the day are the informal relationships that can rise above the silo mentality. It would be likely that the other person would be flexible and helpful. The alternative might well be a firm rebuff.

Another example of the importance of relationship is from the service end of an organization 'in relation' to management. We have noted many times, as we am sure you have, when asking for something unusual, "I'm sorry, I only work here, and they're the rules" when it is obvious that, for us, the rules are not working. If we can make some comment that might be useful, we might suggest passing on such information. We might well be met with horror or a shrug – "after all we only work here – and look what happened last time someone told the boss...". But what if the relationship between employees and their managers was sound and open? Important information could be passed on freely. Not only that but, it may well impact on management enough to re-examine the rule in question and its current value. This, in turn, could effect a change. The result could well be improved performance. Relationships have the capability to deliver flexibility and adaptability whereas to achieve these within rules means interpreting them 'flexibly'. This is a contradiction that most of us have, at some time, embraced in order to get the job done.

From a psychological perspective, relationships are developed more effectively when a person 'knows' him or herself in a relational way. When we are aware of what we think, how we feel, what things make us act as we do, and what we need in our interactions, then we can communicate in a way that is true to ourselves. When we can be open and honest with ourselves we can be the same with others.

In recent years, writers like Goleman, Boyatzis & McKee have contributed in the area of emotional intelligence. They talk in terms of emotional maturity and competencies demonstrated in Table 5.1 below and have developed assessment tools to determine strengths and areas for development.

**PERSONAL COMPETENCE**: These capabilities determine how we manage ourselves.

**SELF AWARENESS**
- Emotional self-awareness: Reading one's own emotions and recognizing their impact; using "gut sense" to guide decisions
- Accurate self-assessment: Knowing one's strengths and limits
- Self Confidence: A sound sense of one's self-worth and capabilities

**SELF-MANAGEMENT**
- Emotional self-control: Keeping disruptive emotions and impulses under control
- Transparency: Displaying honesty and integrity; trustworthiness
- Adaptability: The drive to improve performance to meet inner standards of excellence
- Initiative: Readiness to act and seize opportunities
- Optimism: Seeing the upside in events

**SOCIAL COMPETENCE**: These capabilities determine how we manage relationships.

**SOCIAL AWARENESS**
- Empathy: Sensing other's emotions, understanding their perspective, and taking active interest in their concerns
- Organizational awareness: Reading the currents, decision networks, and politics at the organizational level
- Service: Recognizing and meeting follower, client, or customer needs

**RELATIONSHIP MANAGEMENT**
- Inspirational leadership: Guiding and motivating with a compelling vision
- Influence: Wielding a range of tactics for persuasion
- Developing others: Bolstering others' abilities through feedback and guidance
- Change catalyst: Initiating, managing, and leading in a new direction
- Conflict management: Resolving disagreements
- Building bonds: Cultivating and maintaining a web of relationships
- Teamwork and collaboration: Cooperation and team building

**Table 5.1 The Emotional Competence Framework**

You will note that there are two 'domains' – Personal Competence and Social Competence. These focus on the ability to relate first of all to self and then to others.

Other writers like Cooper and Sawaf[31] claim that emotional intelligence is a key factor in business success. They sum it up using 'four cornerstones' (Table 5.2).

---

**1st Cornerstone - Emotional Literacy**

1. *emotional honesty*
2. *emotional energy*
3. *emotional feedback*
4. *practical intuition*

**2nd Cornerstone - Emotional Fitness**

5. *authentic presence*
6. *trust radius*
7. *constructive discontent*
8. *resilience and renewal*

**3rd Cornerstone - Emotional Depth**

11. *unique potential and purpose*
12. *commitment*
13. *applied integrity*
14. *influence without authority*

**4th Cornerstone - Emotional Alchemy**

15. *intuitive flow*
16. *reflective time-shifting*
17. *opportunity sensing*
18. *creating the future*

---

**Table 5.2 Four Cornerstones of Emotional Intelligence**

---

[31] Cooper, R. & Sawaf, A. (1997) *Executive EQ. Emotional Intelligence in Business.* London, Butler and Tanner.

These key attributes help the leader to recognise that, in order to build constructive relationships, qualities such as self and other awareness, earning and giving respect, taking and giving responsibility are elements of connectivity. We would add the need for authenticity (our workshop participants usually call this by a variety of names including integrity and honesty). Integrity and purpose are two qualities for which employees possess a special radar.

Deep and informed 'people skills' are, we propose, needed in times of uncertainty. Where leaders have technical skills also, this makes a powerful combination. It is interesting that when we ask successful leaders whether they would rather hire technical experts who were not so good with people or candidates who were good with people but not so good technically, the answer is usually the same. 'We can always buy technical skills to support the person, but if he or she does not have a clue about people then we would not dare take the risk.' As we say this, we are reminded of the many management roles that are filled using only technical competency as a criterion. Again, following our 'both/and' approach we would add the relational criterion. The concept of meaning becomes expanded now. As well as being technical, meaning needs to be constructed and interpreted in relation to people. Here we see a duality emerging of technical and emotional areas that the leader can draw down on when assessing a situation. Newcomers to university life, we understand, are required to become as familiar with theories about relationships and emotional competence as they are about analytical and statistical techniques.

The need to invest in developing relationships cannot be overstated. In our own work with organizations we have conducted major programs to develop areas where relationships play a central role. Communication, team development, team dynamics, leadership and understanding individual differences, and thinking about organizations as living systems all have this aim. Where some of these things have been done before and the framework has been passive and instructional, they buttress the control concept and validate traditional management style. Where, in contrast, they are action and learning oriented, allowing challenge and disagreement, they are more resonant with participative management style. We discussed in chapter three some of the shortcomings of the ways in which we produce detailed plans and budgets. Here, we address the issue again and introduce two ideas, of flexibility and guidance.

### Flexible Budgets to Guide

Have you ever been on the tip of something really great – an innovative idea that could shape the future of the organization? You take it to your boss to get support and she responds, 'I like it, but it is not in the budget.'

That response signals problems far greater than personal frustration. Stewart writes:[32]

> Budgets, say experts, control the wrong things, like head count, and miss the right ones, such as quality, customer service – and even profits. Worse they erect walls between the various parts of the company and between a company and its customers. A.T. Kearney consultant Robert Gunn says, 'When you're controlled by a budget, you're not controlling the business.'

Examples like this are common from our experience, and signal that the focus of the organization has more to do with limitation than seeking opportunities. When budgets become management's main tool in achieving performance they can distort long term planning and prevent flexibility in use of resources. The focus on budgets can distort organizational performance by people doing things that are not in the best interests of the organization, especially if meeting budget is linked to incentive pay. Budgets can become an end in themselves.

Detailed plans and budgets are useful in terms of tracking where the money has gone and may be of some use when our organizations exist in a world that is close to certainty and agreement and, where tomorrow will be like yesterday and growth is not a target. However, when organizations are far from certainty and agreement, the best that we can have are broad plans and guiding budgets.

Have you ever wondered why there is low commitment to the budgeting and planning process in organizations? Perhaps, deep down,

---

[32] Stewart, Thomas.A (1990) *Why Budgets are Bad for Business*. Fortune, June 4, (p179).

we know that for many of us it is a futile exercise. We know that we will encounter the unexpected. The budgeting and planning process will be of little use to us in dealing with the unexpected.

When we develop broad strategic plans and budgets we need to understand that, as we face uncertainty, we will need to adapt and modify those plans and budgets. Remember that the budget game is the result of trying to control negative behaviour, like spending too much, while largely ignoring the positive behaviours that build the business. Budgets may show what we spend on customer service, but not what value customers put on that service.

There is a deep desire in each of us to be able to predict and plan with high levels of accuracy, but in reality, the thought that we can always achieve certainty and predictability is a fantasy. What we need to value is our ability to respond flexibly to situations where we are far from certainty and agreement.

What we need to measure is outputs and not inputs. Many budgets force people to control how much their operation spends and ignore how much it earns.

A major tension facing us at this point is that the world in which the organization exists wants certainty and predictability. However, the management of the business knows that it faces uncertainty and variability, which can only be responded to with flexibility and a preparedness to be adaptable.

## Communities of Practice, Networks and Partnerships

As soon as we leave bureaucratic formal structures and methods behind, we also leave the world of rigidly defined relationships. We can replace the 'mechanically' constructed and defined relationships with those that are closer to the three we talk about here. The first is a community of practice.

## Communities of Practice

Organizations that depend on knowledge are taking new forms – communities of practice. Two concepts come together here, community and practice. A community of practice is a group of people informally bound together by shared expertise and a passion for joint enterprise. Communities of practice galvanize knowledge sharing, learning and change. Here's how Wegner, Mc Dermott, & Snyder[33] describe them:

> Communities of practice are groups of people who come together to share and learn from one another face-to-face and virtually. They are held together by a common interest in a body of knowledge and are driven by a desire and need to share problems, experiences, insights, templates, tools, and best practices. As other authors have pointed out, community members deepen their knowledge by interacting on an ongoing basis, and over time, develop a set of shared practices.

People form them for a variety of reasons – to maximize connections with peers, to respond to external changes, or to meet new challenges when the organization's strategy changes. Members inevitably share knowledge in free flowing creative ways that foster new approaches to problems. Communities of practice can drive strategies, generate new opportunities, solve problems, promote the spread of best practices, develop peoples' competencies and help recruit and retain talent.

The paradox of such communities is that although they are usually self-organizing and thus resistant to external control and interference, they do require specific leadership efforts to develop them and to integrate them into an organization. Only when they can be integrated into an organization can they contribute effectively to the success of that organization. The leader who can successfully do this is one who can recognise and appreciate the power of community in the workplace and also the power of sharing.

### Networks

Networks are collections of people who may or may not share the same expertise or professional interest but appreciate the dependency that they have on one another. Networks may comprise

[33] Wegner, E, Mc Dermott, R, Snyder, W.M. (2002) *Cultivating Communities of Practice* Boston, Harvard University Press.

people with quite different skill sets and doing quite different jobs. Their dependency on each other is the glue that holds them together.

Networks provide a variety of support services. One is 'intelligence' in the form of a wide range of unique knowledge. They can act as a sort of shadow bureaucracy so that red tape can be avoided. They are not attached to any hierarchies of decision-making, quite the reverse. Network members come and go and they are valued for the very different contributions they make. There are situations where these qualities are easily expressed such as the one below. The point we want to make is that networks (if they are allowed to be) are a valuable asset to everyday working life.

Here is our example. Imagine that you are held hostage by terrorists in a building. An elite army corps is called in to secure your release. If the soldiers had to work through the bureaucratic channels of the army organization to obtain information on things like the water supply, power supply, air conditioning systems etc. before initiating action, you can guess what would happen. What do they actually do? They use their networks to provide the intelligence needed to respond quickly. Rapid and up-to-date responses are made possible because the people are not shackled by formal methods and structures.

## Partnerships

Partnerships are often talked about but not always well understood. The concept is a 'we' thing. Relationships that are defined in terms of customer and supplier, boss and subordinate do not convey this 'we' quality. In a partnership, each person knows that his/her success is interdependent with the success of others. A partnership depends on an evenly shared distribution of power.

In fact, it is a win/win situation where the basis of the relationship is not to win at the other party's expense. One party can only gain if the other does as well. One definition that we have heard is that *partnerships are where each party is passionate about the others' profits.*

In one of our consulting arrangements, we were working with teams that worked in continuous shift patterns. We helped them to build very robust relationships *within* the various shift teams. However, as is a perennial problem in shift situations, the relationship *between* the teams was problematic. Two major problems were a blame culture and a win/lose approach. We used some of the ideas we have talked about here. We constructed the targets and goals with each team in a way that would set up the next shift for success. This recognised the inter-dependencies that needed to exist between shifts and created a partnership approach to operating the plant.

To exercise extraordinary leadership requires us to move from a reliance on bureaucratic structures where the relationships between people are rigidly defined, to partnerships where the people define them together. Rigid structures are useful to us when our organizations exist in an environment that is close to certainty and we are in agreement as to how to respond to changes. Remember though that a reliance on rigid rules and structures is an expression of a very deep and strong desire to achieve equilibrium, stability and safety. Perhaps striving for equilibrium makes us feel more secure and safe. Having a defined rigid structure does just that – but let's not forget that whilst it provides us with the *fantasy* of security and safety, it simultaneously makes us feel trapped or imprisoned.

To embrace partnerships takes courage and trust since both information and power have to be shared.

### Learning and Not Blame

As we have previously mentioned, one of the most destructive things we can do to our organization is to create a culture of blame. Blame is the product of errors in the organization that are not looked upon as learning opportunities but as excuses to find a culprit. The fear of being blamed will increase over time. People will play safe, not speak up and not present risky information. This limits and skews (in favour of the uncritical) the information available to the organization. This, in turn, leads to failure to successfully solve problems and make good decisions. This cycle of failure will attract more blame and so the value of 'avoiding blame' will be reinforced.

We have found that errors cause cover-ups because people are unwilling to take risks. We can recall a story from a client, where suddenly the production line stopped. No information was forthcoming and everyone close to the problem behaved as if they were totally unaware of the cause. They offered no data and no suggestions. The management immediately commissioned a team of engineers to investigate the cause of the problem and find a solution. After a week of intensive investigation, the cause could not be identified. Later, in a team-building workshop, a production employee admitted that he had accidentally shut the line down but was not prepared to admit it because of the blame and punishment culture that existed. The real cost to the organization was not this single incident although this was bad enough. It was the cost associated with constant risk avoidance and the fear to speak up. We often hear the saying 'no names – no pack drill'.

Eventually, a culture of blame and punishment damages the relationships between people and trust breaks down completely. People become cynical about the organization's published beliefs and values and respond to what they believe to be the real values (that is those that match managements' behaviours). The result is that people just don't care – 'who gives a .......!' becomes the prevailing attitude. The result is even poorer decision-making, more errors and more blame and punishment[34].

The blame and punishment culture seems to produce people who choose to be victims. We say 'people who choose to be' because we think it's important to state the difference between a true victim and one who chooses to be a victim – they are two very different things, with the latter causing a state of victim mentality. Examples of true victims are those who have been subjected to unprovoked violence, brutality or rape – actions totally outside the victims' control.

Victims of blame are those who choose to see situations they face to be clearly the result of actions by others. They become helpless and do not take any responsibility for negative outcomes. This highly dependent behaviour creates a need for rescuers – people to save them. Unfortunately, rescuers soon become persecutors because 'victims by choice' need to feel that they are persecuted in order to maintain their victim status. The rescuer also highlights and reinforces the incompetence of the victim by solving problems that the victim could not or would not solve. In other words, rescuers

---

[34] We wish to acknowledge a colleague, Liz MacKenzie for introducing us to this thinking through her model of blame.

highlight the victim's inadequacy, sense of dependency and lack of personal responsibility. The antidote is to encourage self-responsibility. Extraordinary leadership is about creating an environment that encourages self-responsibility.

Blame and the fear of punishment drive the culture back to the safety of mechanistic management with its rules and procedures and no need to think and risk being wrong. People are driven to do what they did yesterday because that was safe for them and, they avoided punishment. It also encourages an unquestioning application of rules and procedures. After all, the best way to ensure that tomorrow looks like yesterday is to apply yesterday's rules and procedures. 'We can't get into trouble by applying the rules.' It is a safe strategy in the short term but is potentially dangerous should the organization face increasing uncertainty. This behaviour is anti-learning, anti-change, and anti-empowering. It generates limitation, rather than delivering possibility.

We need to add a piece of caution at this point. We are not suggesting that all mechanistic management is inappropriate. If the features of mechanistic management are used for coherence and direction, mechanistic management could be useful. On the other hand, if rules and regulations are used to support a management style focused on coercion and external control, it serves no positive purpose.

Most of us are used to being judged on whether we made the right decision or not. One of us can recall, at a conference a few years ago, hearing Sir Richard Branson (CEO of Virgin) say that he praised those who made mistakes and could learn from those mistakes. Branson was critical of those who don't make mistakes because they have not learnt or grown.

In traditional organizational life, some of our decisions may not be in the best interest of the organization and our actions can result in mistakes. In such cases, we may spend a lot of time and energy hiding this fact or justifying the original decision. In fact, the unexpected outcome from our decision, could have been the result of an absence of trust. This would impact on the quality of information we could access. Without trust, we would be caught in a self-fulfilling prophecy of failure. Reliable information would not be forthcoming. Under these circumstances, rational problem solving processes would be of little or no use. The unreliability of such rational problem-solving processes as learning methodologies is exaggerated when organizations are facing increasing uncertainty. Typically we avoid the search for error and fail to learn from it.

A culture of learning is where people are encouraged to experiment and innovate. In some ways the current obsession that many organizations have with the quality standards (namely ISO accreditation) is the opposite of learning since it ensures that organizations become 'frozen' by past and present practices. Furthermore, when organizations are far from certainty and agreement, how can we be sure that the past is going to be of any use in guiding our future actions? And very often these standards are required for the 'license to operate' we talked about earlier. Standards should be seen as means of achieving valued ends. Many of the quality accreditation processes are seen as ends in themselves instead of tools that provide the means to achieving the desired ends of a quality culture that is continuously learning. Of course this does not necessarily have to be the case. It depends a lot on the mental model or paradigm of the manager/leader.

We talked about mental models and paradigms earlier. One particular change is to what is often referred to as double loop learning[35]. Double loop learning differs from the single loop that exists in mechanistic management. Single loop learning assesses where actual performance sits in relation to the target. Perhaps it is best illustrated by an example. If you consider the cruise control mechanism in a motorcar that is set at 100 km/h., then the engine management system will control the speed of the engine to achieve the speed target. Here a simple linear relationship exists around the speed target.

On the other hand, how does one know if the speed target is appropriate? It is one thing to set the speed and another thing entirely to judge what should be set in a variety of changing circumstances. We enter a 60 km/h speed zone. Will we stay at 100 km/h? We see what is happening on the road. We remind ourselves of the law. We make a judgment. This is an example of double-loop learning. The double loop goes a bit deeper and engages in thinking about the appropriateness of the speed target to its environment.

---

[35] Argyris,C. (1989) *Reasoning, Learning and Action* San Francisco, Jossey-Bass.

Triple loop learning goes one level deeper still. It is systemic and often holistic in nature. We might take the idea of speed and cars and the consequences on the environment that we pass on to future generations. We might graduate to the one about being a good corporate citizen.

What is needed is a culture that accepts that, in an environment of uncertainty, not all experiments will be successful. People often say that managers get what they reward. If they reward experiments even if they fail (as long as learning is gained) they will get a positive attitude toward trying again. If they punish failures (whether there is learning or not), they will get a negative attitude to anything remotely smacking of risk and experimentation. The culture needs to reward those willing to take risks to innovate. In fact, when we are far from certainty and far from agreement, there is no map, no formula, and no plan. No one has been there before and we are pioneers. Every step becomes an opportunity to learn and grow in the organization. This increases the intangible value of the organization.

> **The culture needs to reward those willing to take risks to innovate.**

Where change is the opened-ended type, managers are ignorant of the outcomes that might flow from their decisions. This is both frightening and exhilarating. Cause/effect relationships cannot be predicted since they are facing totally new situations. Clearly, taught solutions that result from past experiences are obsolete and, probably, most of the thinking that led to them. The way forward is to foster transformational learning that is learning built on potentials and innovative thinking.

> **Promote learning that is built on potentials and innovative thinking.**

Collingridge[36] introduced an interesting and challenging set of ideas around decision-making. He suggested that effective decision-making

---

[36] Collingridge, D. (1980) *The Social Control of Technology* Milton Keynes, Open University Press.

when one is far from certainty, and there is little or no agreement, is a search for error and a willingness to learn from what is discovered. Normally, people apply rational processes that would involve searching for the right answer. However, Collingridge argues that people should choose an option that can most easily be found to be in error - error that can be most easily corrected. In doing this you close off fewer options and you get more opportunities to adjust to changing situations and possibly develop more than one right answer.

## Discovery

Discovery is an interesting concept. Like creativity and innovation, many organizations know that they need to be discovering rather than repeating. They want to be inimitable and, given the ability to buy similar technology and software systems, they recognise that personal intelligence and creativity are very hard to imitate. However, people who want to discover things do not want to be punished for it. There are some 'unseen' punishments designed into our performance management systems. We ask people to perform to targets and goals. We do this within set periods of time. The targets and goals need to be at least tangible so that it can be ascertained that they have been reached. These methods of setting performance goals and monitoring them are an inherited part of the distant past when bureaucratic organizing rested on the idea that the person would function according to a structure (such as a structured performance management system). Discovery requires moving outside of the functional and structural box. It has no targets or goals. It has no time frame. Discoveries are sometimes tangible and sometimes not. What we are saying here is that discovery within a well integrated and structured performance management system is like putting a round (or shapeless) peg into a square hole.

So what do we recommend? Well, we need to remember that we are not working with a blank slate here. People are products of organizational learning. If performing to instructions has been very well rewarded in the past then the first thing the leader needs to see to is managing unlearning. As we said earlier, some disturbance or tension needs to happen to dislodge the old ways of thinking. This can be very uncomfortable for both the learners and the leaders, and it is here that encouragement and faith in learners' abilities is needed.

In other words, we need to know what we are asking of people to leave their comfort zones of certainty. We need to make sure that the journey to new thinking and discovery is rewarded, *whether or not tangible discoveries are made*. The exercise of discovery is valued for its brave and sometimes bizarre thinking. Sometimes this pays off with an outcome or a product and sometimes, the most one can say is that it is an exercise in 'white water' thinking.

There are no patterns to discovery thinking either. People need to be placed in a position where they are able to discover what they need for their own unique situations. We recognise that individuals learn at different rates. Where organizations want new ideas and innovation, new ways of thinking need to be encouraged. We can offer two practical examples of how we would support discovery thinking. We will also suggest some conditions essential to this enterprise.

Friday is discovery day. For one hour sometime during the day the team will organize itself to get sufficient cover to meet for one hour to do 'white water' thinking. (Note that favours may be owed and collected all over the place as colleagues are needed to cover essential jobs. An immediate improvement in fractured relationships is called for.) The only expectation is that there are no presentations and the modus operandi is argument and challenge. The golden rule here is, of course, it is the issue not the person that is challenged. Havoc is OK. Shouting, arguing, over-talking is OK. Whatever. The hour is self controlled and self organized. The team decides if and when anything is reported from the session. Leaders are responsible for keeping faith with the arrangements, not looking for any measurable outcomes and being willing, if called upon to produce (and pay for) any expert advice requested by the team. The second golden rule is a willingness to listen to new ideas, and either resource them or meet with the team and present an argument as to why something cannot happen.

A variation on this idea is where there are no formal arrangements but there is an understanding that if someone in the team is excited about a new idea or method, the team will be able to call on cover so that an impromptu session can be held. The teams themselves can constitute a 'steering group' selected from themselves and other teams in other departments. The membership changes regularly and voluntarily. Any discoveries are talked through to see whether they can be of benefit to the larger group. The steering group can fulfil another function. It can throw problems experienced in one team open to anyone else's teams and ask for some creative solutions that might be tried. Leadership support for this design is to allow and honour the need for time and expertise as decided by the teams and not managers. Leaders and managers will feel the most pressure to live with uncertainty as there will be no way of knowing when discovery will occur.

Discovery entails moving as far from certainty as possible. It means moving away from the desire to give people a formula or map. The route to discovery is travelled in engagement with others. Feedback is once again important but it is a different form from the official feedback at appraisal interviews. The most important feedback is happening informally and conversationally.

The most valuable thing a leader can do is to promote and reward a learning culture. This is the antithesis of the blame culture that we hear so much about in organizations. It takes courage in a leader to reward a drop in performance. Yet as we show in Figure 5.4, most discovery entails the learner going down what we call the U shaped curve. You can see that the learner is at the stage of excellence. He is highly pleased with his expertise and skills and the esteem they bring from others. Entering the discovery mode (rather than the continuous improvement one) has the effect of knocking him off his expert perch. He feels gauche and somewhat stupid as he reaches for the unknown. The excellent performance has competition from the new learning struggle so it is likely that it goes down to some degree. Now the learner and the leader are in an unusual position. The learner is experiencing frustration, perhaps self-doubt and one or more failures along the way. These are almost forgotten sensations. The leader is in the position of providing support and encouragement for something that might or might not become a worthwhile discovery. Also, she will be, by traditional standards, rewarding poor performance. At the very least, we see the need to make the notion of performance more than just outcome oriented. We need to both measure outcomes and support learning exercises where the process of thinking creatively is seen as an end in itself and a way of expressing some of the organization's cumulative intelligence.

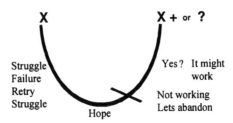

**Figure 5.4 Supporting Learning**

**Performance Management from a Broad Base**

Traditional performance management processes are 'top down', that is, the person in the hierarchical level above controls the process. This approach may be useful providing the person above is technically competent to make judgements of the individual's performance and they are able to plan performance levels during the following accounting period. When organizations are far from certainty, this level of planning is not possible. Also, it is essential when facing uncertainty and when far from agreement, that information on performance is broadly based. Sources of information on performance should include customers, peers, bosses and members of the team that are the recipients of the individual's services.

There is another dilemma. That is, whether the performance management process is individually focused or team focused. Traditionally, measurement is focused on the individual. This only encourages self-interest. Self-interest is displayed by withholding information when promotion relies on an individual's skill and knowledge. Here we see how important systems are in supporting the values proposition.

However, in reality, there are very few individuals who can claim their success or otherwise to be the result of their individual effort. More likely it will be the result of a collective effort. After all, the complexity of the organization requires many people to work together to enable it to perform. High levels of interdependency exist between individuals and between the tasks performed.

Many performance management systems tend to focus on quantitative outcomes, for example, sales completed, tonnes produced, costs per tonne, claims processed, lost time injuries, etc. Such targets may be suspect when the organization is facing uncertainty. Today doesn't look like yesterday so comparisons with the past may be meaningless. There are too many confounding variables to consider them valid or reliable.

Secondly, if we are trying to build a culture that focuses on the process to ensure performance, we need to have measures that encourage people and teams to focus on the ways of achieving those tangible outcomes.

Organizations that wish to be managed by values in order to optimise performance must be prepared to measure or evaluate in a way congruent with those values. It makes sense that people pay attention to what is being measured and choose strategies to ensure their outputs and behaviour are in alignment with what is being measured. The old saying that 'what is of interest to my boss fascinates me' applies.

**Information Model of Organization**

In chapter three, we described the organizational design that best suited the needs of mechanistic management. This was the bureaucratic model. To lead in an extraordinary way, the scaffolding of structures, rules, regulations and procedures needs to be replaced by some other device to bring the organization together. We have selected information for this role and we see organizations as dynamic and generative creators of information in an environment where no one has the monopoly and everyone's information contribution is a valued piece of intellectual property.

We know that information is equally well valued in the mechanistic and the extraordinary framework. Yet there is a world of difference in the two interpretations of the word.

To mechanistic managers, information is often about right answers. Very often we have seen mechanistic managers limit access to information because of a 'need to know' mentality. It is often evident that those at the bottom of the food chain do not need to know much at all. As we explain later, information in a mechanistic world hopes for validation and certainty. As they say in the quality movement 'facts not rumours'. The tone was set in traditional versions of information systems where it was possible to construct a DFD, data flow diagram. This would be used to map the flow of information in a sequential way. As Champy[37] found in his later work, the use of information by mechanistic managers did not help the leadership cause.

To extraordinary leaders information is seen very differently. We see it as more of a swirl, a flow, a stream of ideas and experiences. In terms of new information, this can (some would say must) come from the flux of chaos where randomness generates new order. We agree absolutely with Wheatley's[38] comment that, 'The fuel of life is new information – novelty – ordered into new structures. We need to have information coursing through our systems, disturbing the peace, imbuing everything it touches with new life.' The sharing of this sort of information is crucial to organizations performing in an extraordinary way. If increasing uncertainty is being experienced, there is a need to have fast and reliable processes for gathering, analysing and sharing information and intelligence. Returning to the jazz theme, we envisage a steady stream of factual information whilst new and generative information happens within the relationships and activities that are constantly developing and changing. Information is the life-blood of the organization and as Meg Wheatley says, it is as important as currency to an economy. If we expect rapid and dynamic responses to the issues faced by the organization, information needs to be readily accessible to those required to respond. In fact, it could be said that the only role of managers is to facilitate the gathering and analysis of information and to provide feedback processes.

---

[37] Champy, J. (1995) *Reengineering management: The mandate for new leadership* London, Harper Collins.
[38] Wheatley, M.J. (1994) *Leadership and the New Science; Learning about Organizational from an Orderly Universe* San Francisco, Berrett-Koehler (p105).

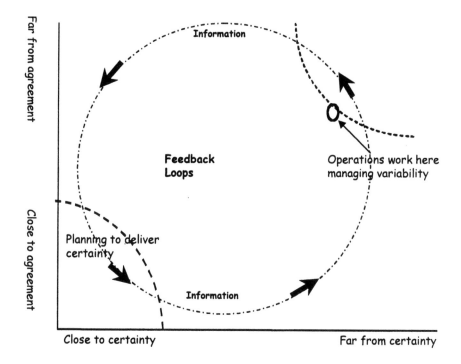

## Figure 5.5 Feedback of Information

Once again, we do not see any one approach as 'the winner'. There is a place for tangible, factual 'certain' information just as there is a place for that based on connectedness and iteration, with no guarantee that the information will be certain tomorrow. We demonstrate this in Figure 5.5 where we see both extraordinary leadership and mechanistic management working together via feedback loops between areas of uncertainty and certainty. This needs to be a continuing cyclic process. As Champy[39] says though, in order to work together in harmony, mechanistic managers at least need to appreciate 'the other sort' of information.

---

[39] Champy, J. (1995) *Reengineering management: The mandate for new leadership* London, Harper Collins.

Working within the zone or area of uncertainty and far from agreement we tend to see information as more of a river, sometimes a turbulent one, than as containers of facts, figures and reports. These are very useful though when the management task is to keep information contained and under control. Wheatley[40] has an interesting way of looking at this, when she talks about 'information chastity belts' being applied by managers. In spite of the best attempts at controlling information, there is little doubt that there is a strong self-organizing element to it. Information sets out. It meets people. They attach pieces of personal interpretation and even facts to it and then the information goes on its way, into another feedback loop where new recipients add a little of their own organizing to the information. There has been an increasing ambiguity happening around the information that started out quite clearly. The information has become complex instead of simple.

We propose that in turning a blind eye to the flux and randomness that can overtake information, or even worse, taking steps to shut it out, organizations will function with a reduced information supply. It is possible to do this (just) providing its circumstances place it close to certainty and agreement. In these circumstances, the traditional hierarchical structures that limit the information collected and distributed, can survive, albeit in an impoverished way. It is when circumstances change and suddenly turbulence happens that the lack of generative and complex information will be felt. In the worse case scenario, the organization's information systems may be so blinkered that they may not even be aware that change has hit.

It is important to talk about two different information processes of an organization. The first is that which flows around the system. The second is that information that comes into the organization from the outside world. This is sometimes referred to as 'intelligence'. When organizations exercise extraordinary leadership, it is essential that as much information as is known is rapidly shared amongst all involved in the business of the organization. This can be quite an experience for employees, when suddenly they are 'part of the intelligence network for the business.' For information to be shared it is essential that robust and trusting relationships exist,

---

[40] Wheatley, M.J. (1994) *Leadership and the New Science; Learning about Organizational from an Orderly Universe* San Francisco, Berrett-Koehler (p105).

otherwise the only information shared will be that which is deemed to be politically safe. Obviously, in these circumstances a great deal of useful information is lost.

It is intriguing that organizations embark on expensive and time consuming programs to increase problem solving and decision-making capabilities yet ignore or underplay the need to foster robust relationships with the view to fostering a climate for voluntary sharing of information. For example, we know that when we bring people together in new ways, information can be seen in new ways too. That information is often crucial to the problem or decision to be made. However, if relationships are not attended to then the activity would be like having several telephones with no connecting line. As most of us have found out, connectivity helps information flow and it in turn depends on trusting relationships.

Typically, hierarchical structures are full of ways to restrict and inhibit information creation and flow. They have restricted points of entry for information from outside. The information that comes to boards of directors, chief executives, chief officers or 'important' people in marketing and public relations usually flows around this restricted space, somewhere out of orbit from the spinning organization. It is not difficult to imagine how much organization intelligence is lost here. When practicing extraordinary leadership there are several things to bear in mind. One is that an environment needs to be created so that information can be iterative. Restrictions that stop information from feeding back on itself in new ways need to be lifted. Once people get hold of information it becomes an interpretation. Information as facts (such as we see in International Standards Office, ISO processes) is seen as only one of many kinds of information. It may be that the leader has to intervene to produce a disturbance in the interests of releasing new and creative energy that, in turn, appears as new information. Above all, information is a community activity. All employees of the organization need to be actively involved in creating and gathering intelligence. The search for this often means that the leader has to support and encourage dissent and contradiction from which new information or old information seen in a new way, emerges. This activity characterizes the extraordinary leader in the same way that providing chains of command for information to travel characterised the mechanistic manager.

Increasing uncertainty demands that many types of information are needed to enable, not only rapid, but creative responses to issues.

We are reminded of a recent story from a client who produces sheet metal for further manufacturing. One particular customer required the removal of oil spots on the steel. Accordingly, the production line was always thoroughly washed. To do this, the manufacturing process had to be shut down at a considerable cost. During a visit to the customer by a group of production workers (who actually produce the product for that customer), the workers discovered that the customer could cope with some minor amounts of oil on the sheet at the beginning of the coil of steel. Therefore, the need to thoroughly clean the production line was not necessary since any residue oil was quickly eliminated. This led to considerable cost savings for the business. This intelligence would not have surfaced if the entry points had not been expanded enabling people involved to have access to the customer along with trusting relationships with the plant managers. If this particular information had been sought (which would have been unlikely) it would have resided in the marketing department or with senior managers who, in turn, might have restricted information about what is and what isn't possible on the production line. Direct communication in this instance paid off. The sharing of information is an essential, active part of the process of developing relationships. From this develops a sense of identity. In fact, information is the keystone in the organizational arch, on which extraordinary leadership depends.

In part one of this chapter, we brought you a different view of organizational rules, structures, detailed plans, rational processes, learning, performance management from above and the bureaucratic model (which becomes the information model in the extraordinary setting). In part two, we continue to share our ideas on extraordinary leadership.

Chapter Five
- Part two -

# EXTRAORDINARY LEADERSHIP

In part one, we took elements from mechanistic management and showed what they might look like within the extraordinary leadership mindset.

In part two, we talk about elements (Figure 5.6) that are important but not, we think, taken seriously within a mechanistic management framework.

## "EXTRAORDINARY" LEADERSHIP

## Performance = Direction + Willingness

-Vision & values

-Trust & support

-Identity & purpose

-Personal responsibility

-Customer focused

**Figure 5.6 Extraordinary Leadership in Action - Part 2**

**Vision and Values**

To us, vision and values provide the personal and social glue that holds the organization together. The adoption of extraordinary leadership is a decision to lead by vision and values. The vision is a series of statements about how the stakeholders in the organization would like to see it operating. Visions are usually idealistic statements that focus on the future. Like the word vision suggests, it is the act of looking ahead.

Values are about the deep images in our culture that drive behaviour and decisions. The statement of values is an expression of our shared norms and beliefs. The values and beliefs govern the way in which we interact with one another, our customers, shareholders and society in general.

> *Values are among the most stable and enduring characteristics of individuals. They are the basis upon which attitudes and personal preferences are formed. They are the basis for crucial decisions, life directions and personal tastes; much of what we are is a product of the basic values we have developed through our lives. An organization too has a value system, usually referred to as its organizational culture. Research has shown that employees who hold values that are congruent with their organization's values are more productive and satisfied. Holding values that are inconsistent with company values, on the other hand, is a major source of frustration, conflict and non-productivity.[41]*

In the book on managing change through core values[42] Alma said:

> *The values expressed in the vision form the mental model or paradigm of 'the things it is legitimate to do around here'. Vision represents a stable, future-looking value system, which dictates appropriate and approved behaviours. The vision governs methods of doing business, methods of interacting in the workplace and methods of relating to outside forces. The expectations are that the negotiated values will be upheld in daily transactional business.*

The bureaucratic mindset produces a vision of its own. It already has values embedded within it. These are *control* and *objectivity*. It is

---

[41] Whetton, D. and Cameron, K.S. (1991) *Developing Management Skills, 2nd edition* New York, Harper & Row.
[42] Whiteley, A. (1995) *Managing Change – a Core Values Approach.* South Melbourne: MacMillan Educational Pty Ltd.

these values, these (theoretically) shared values that led to mechanistic view of people and the scientific way of managing them.

We asked:

> *Do workers actually value control? Do they value mechanizing all aspects of their jobs? Do workers value dependency as managers think for them? In many 'core-value' workshops ... not once have these values been given. Examples of values which are generated unfailingly are honesty and honest feedback, integrity, loyalty, commitment, mutual respect, recognition, customer focus, creativity and autonomy/giving me the freedom to do things my way.*

A major tension develops when organizations say that they want to be driven by publicly stated values but behave in ways that are clearly contradictory to those published values. For example, many of the rules put in place within organizations are underpinned by the value that people can't be trusted and need to be placed under close scrutiny and external control. How often do we see trust and honesty appearing in the organization's list of values? Or more tellingly, how often do we see those practiced even when they are stated? Behaving in a way that differs from the stated values is a violation of integrity. It is no wonder that often employees laugh when they look at the nicely presented 'vision and values' statement displayed openly on the wall. This tension between what is promised and what is found in practice is a major cause of mistrust in organizations.

If we are to reduce the dependency on rules and regulations, it is necessary to replace them (not overlay them) with an agreed set of values that will govern the behaviour of people in the organization. To manage by values is a very powerful way of managing. For those who do not 'live' the values there should be consequences. Sanctions within teams and groups would be far more powerful and far reaching than any that could be applied through the rules framework. As we have said all the way through this conversation, rules are externally imposed controls that require energy, time and money to apply. They deliver rigidity and allow for the repetition of yesterday's actions and behaviours. Rules are about imitation and limitation.

Control from within the system via personal values is far reaching, particularly in areas which are new and as such do not yet have rules to apply. Let's take an example when an employee is faced with a situation that hasn't arisen before. She is faced with a dilemma. There is no rule to guide her. After all, there are only so many rules. If there isn't a rule, is the rule to do nothing? What is she to do? If however, she is guided by the values of the organization which have personal meaning for her this will be her guide in whatever (infinite) number of situations that might arise. We'd like to share this experience with you.

**Rules driven employee story**

Customer: *Hi, I'd like to place an urgent order totalling around $10,000 but I need it by tomorrow!*
Employee: *I'm sorry, but I can't get it to you by tomorrow, our deliveries have already gone out for the day, and we're backlogged, so the earliest I can get them to you is in three days.*
Customer: *Look, what about a private courier?*
Employee: *I'm sorry, but we don't use private couriers, it's company policy!*
Customer: *Yes, but I have one and I'm happy to pay for it myself.*
Employee: *I'm sorry, I'd like to be able to help you, but they're the rules, I can't change them, I only work here.*
Customer: *Yes I see, but if I picked them up personally that would be OK wouldn't it?*
Employee: *Oh yes, that would be fine.*
Customer: *Well, I can't because I have other commitments, so what's the difference if I just send a courier instead of me to pick them up?*
Employee: *Look, I told you - they're the rules, we're not allowed to deal with outside couriers - and I can't do anything about it.*

Assuming that customer service and satisfaction is taken seriously in an organization, perhaps the following would be more useful.

**Values driven employee story**

Customer: *Hi, I'd like to place an urgent order totalling around $10,000 but I need it by tomorrow!*

Employee: *I'm sorry, but I can't get it to you by tomorrow, our deliveries have already gone out for the day, and we're backlogged, so the earliest I can get them to you is in three days.*
Customer: *Look, what about a private courier?*
Employee: *I'm sorry, but we don't have any arrangement with private couriers!*
Customer: *Yes, but I have one and I'm happy to pay for it myself.*
Employee: *Well, in that case, if you organize it all, including pick up and payment, I can't see why we can't help you out. I'd be happy to take your order.*

Here's an analogy that Stacey[43] uses. Think of snowflakes. The number of different snowflakes sizes are infinite, all reacting differently to the environment as they fall to the ground. Yet they are all still true to the initial conditions or basic set-up of snowflakes. Why can we not have infinite variety and yet be true to a particular (organizational) design? There really is no reason that we can see.

Let us apply the snowflake idea to organizational life. The initial conditions that are stable and enduring are the values. The worker may have to react to situations in a variety of ways. Yet s/he has the ability (and permission) to respond to all kinds of different circumstances because the values anchor the behaviour. In doing this from a values perspective, she also develops a sense of personal responsibility (rather than separate to the policy/rule/company). This then contributes to her sense of identity. Being in tandem with the organization's values may contribute to her sense of belonging, personal value and these in turn may make her willing to exercise her discretion again. In doing so, she is likely to find solutions she hadn't thought of previously. Every time this happens and especially if ideas are shared with others, organizational performance will improve. Should all not go well and remembering our ideas on learning, mistakes would be treated as learning experiences. Learning by personal experience is for many the best kind of learning one can do. It has meaning on a much deeper level, and is not easily forgotten because of the personal nature of the experience.

---

[43] Stacey, R.D. (1996) *Strategic Management & Organizational Dynamics* 2nd Ed London, Pitman.

Values, are internal 'controls' that require no management time, energy or money. Much less time and scarce resources need be applied attending to an organization driven by values. This is because a whole sector of activities disappears from the scene. These are the political and legalistic activities embroiled in efforts to interpret the rules for most personal benefit, perhaps finding loopholes or escape routes so that they do not need to be rigidly followed.

Meg Wheatley[44] stated that, '*If information is the centre stage, then the vision is the field that surrounds the stage.*' Traditionally, we see vision as the place at which we would like to arrive - the destination. We see the vision pulling us towards the future state, operating in a similar way to gravity. It has recently been suggested that the vision is not a destination, but a field that permeates the organization and touches all employees shaping (and being shaped by) their behaviour. Perhaps vision is like a broadcast, pulsing out messages in a way that encourages a good reception. Fields connect people and distant actions. The field of vision allows the separate events or parts in an organization to be pulled together.

Another way to talk about the strange attractor or magnet we talked about earlier is to see it as a field of vision. What is valued stays inside the field and in a self-organized way. If we see each person or group as a microcosm of the organizations 'initial conditions' or essential shape, then we can encourage unique and interesting ways to do things rather than standardized working to formats. We hear mechanistic managers saying, 'What, you want people running around the place like loose cannons?' We would make the response that 'as long as people worked to the values, the only thing that should constrain them is their own creativity, not a set of rules'. We know that those who did not work to the values would not be comfortable. They would not fit and it would be better for them to do something else.

In our work, we have encouraged executive managers to share their vision and values with the workforce, just as the broadcaster does. This is as long as they don't attempt to *enrol* everyone in *their* vision and values. We suggest that it is much more likely that people will

[44] Wheatley, M.J. (1994) *Leadership and the New Science: Learning about Organization from an Orderly Universe* . San Francisco, Berrett-Koehler (p54).

commit to a vision and values that they have had a hand in creating. The values have to be living history and in the core values book Alma talked about culture binding. This is where stories, rituals, heroes and ceremonies are all used to keep the culture alive. Also we see no reason why each team in the organization cannot be encouraged to create its own vision and develop its own values. The golden rule is that they must harmonise with the overarching organizational values and we have found that this occurs almost invariably. The words used to express the vision and values of each team may vary but the spirit and intention must be reflected.

The alignment is more likely to occur if the organization's structures, processes and systems are congruent with the published vision and values. Conversely, if they do not 'match' then a doubt is set up about what is really meant. In our experience, the 'real values' are taken as the ones embedded in the structures, processes and systems as that is where people 'live'. It is hard to retain a commitment to enabling values when these compete with structures that support a bureaucratic view of organizations (control and objectivity). Everyone has to work on behaving in ways that are congruent with the vision and the stated values long after the exciting vision work is done. Such values run deep and we are not usually conscious of them. It is when they are contravened that they come to the fore and unfortunately every time this happens it is a blow to trusting relationships, whether the contravention comes from leaders or employees.

Words and concepts are so powerful. We recall that during a workshop with employees from Dalrymple Bay Coal Terminal, that one of the participants, Steve Bailey, suggested that the organization replace the concept of 'supervision' with 'workervision'. This suggested that there was no dissonance between what the executive wanted for the business and what other employees wanted. His comment also encouraged the group to explore the values that were widely held and the resultant paradigms that developed.

One of our clients has estimated that prior to exercising extraordinary leadership, over 70% of management and supervisory time was spent on dealing with dysfunctional behaviour. It was, he said, caused largely by managing by rules rather than values. Always of interest to employees is the congruency between *what was said* and *what was actually done*. Incongruence produces dysfunction. We suspect that the 70% statistic applies to many organizations.

It is interesting to observe what happens during a major crisis such as an earthquake or a catastrophe in the workplace or simply the collapse of the production process. In these situations, as stated earlier, people automatically deal with events through the application of extraordinary leadership principles. They rely on their relationships with each other. They rely on the rapid sharing of information. They do this within the framework of a clear sense of purpose and identity. They also act within the agreed set of values (both explicit and implicit) and a shared vision. We have now added vision and values as potential components of the organization's *strange attractor*.

One of us can recall becoming quite distressed about people not honouring the finishing time at the end of each workday. The initial response was to enforce the rules - but they were obviously unenforceable. This failure caused a serious questioning of the action taken. After all, if something is not working, do not continue to do it. Try something different. The something different was to focus on developing peoples' commitment to the organization through contribution and service. This in turn was achieved through the development of a sense of identity and shared purpose, rather than the application of the rules. It did not take long for those who had been finishing work earlier than rostered to change their behaviour. Because the management focus was put on contribution rather than finishing time, it meant the employees also focused on contribution rather than finishing time. In other words, they chose to manage the situation by use of the tools of extraordinary leadership, with a particular reliance on the employees identifying with the organization and being committed to the shared purpose, whilst honouring the agreed values of honesty and integrity.

Managing in this extraordinary way yielded greater flexibility from employees and it also demanded greater flexibility from leaders. It allowed for individual needs to be taken into account and for people to respond to the dynamically changing needs of the organization.

Again, if the tools of mechanistic management are of limited use, reliance on relationships, information, purpose and identity, vision and values are essential when facing increasing uncertainty. This leads us to one of the values that always comes top of the list when generating core values - trust. Here we look at trust and support in terms of extraordinary leadership.

## Trust and Support

For many years we have been asking employees "what is the most valued quality of a manager or leader?" Three responses never fail to emerge. At the top of the list is always trust, followed closely by honesty and integrity. It is interesting that over this time, qualities like technical competence, engineering (or accounting or statistical) capability have not made the top three.

Throughout our work we have seen many organizations and their employees busily engaged in improving the performance of the business or the organization. These efforts are usually focused on rational problem solving, the application of engineering and scientific principles, and rational strategies. So often, however, we hear people say, "All that is great for the business. We know that. But what about me?"

We can't recall an organization that does not say that people are its most important asset. Yet it is rare to have that belief addressed at a deep human level. Failure to address this at a deep and authentic level results in people not feeling important. The feeling of not being valued leads to feelings of insecurity, threat, and alienation. In fact, the deeply rooted mechanistic model encourages managers to see people as machines rather than people. In doing so, we apply the same principles of management to people as we do to machines. What a mistake we are making here. Unlike machines that have limited variability, people display infinite variability. When we employ a human being we get a pair of hands plus a mind, including the emotional part we often refer to as the 'heart'. Once again, we bring your attention to the importance of developing emotional competency and in particular social competency as we said in part one of this chapter.

Why do we refuse to see the obvious, particularly when people and their knowledge constitute, in many cases, more than 50% of an organization's total wealth. When people are treated as replaceable parts or as objects to control, inevitably the organization will be filled with frustration, anger and isolation. Poor performance can be expected as a result of destructive political behaviour. The trauma associated with destructive behaviour leads to a complete lack of trust.

There is little mystery around the trust concept and people are remarkably similar when you ask, "If you could not trust me, what would I be doing?" Common answers are, "You would be sharing my confidence with other people, doing one thing and saying another, feeding me a line when the news is bad, so that I am always tensed for a (bad) surprise, going behind my back to get something done, rather than asking me outright" and so on. We mention these because even though responses are similar, one group's examples can not be translated to another group. The dimensions of trust need be defined by people themselves.

The behaviours that demonstrate trustworthiness to us might be different for you. The manager needs to be able to gather (and give) this sort of information so that areas of trust can be agreed upon. In other words, there is a mutuality to trust. Mutual trust is the essence of a high performing organization. Arie de Geus, a former executive of Royal Dutch Shell says, 'In the living company, the essence of the underlying contract is mutual trust.'[45]

To develop robust relationships requires open and honest communication. This in turn, requires trust. Trust is essential if the organization is operating in a zone that is far from certainty where the possibility of complete agreement is low. The old rules and models will be of little use especially as no one is able to provide the formula or recipe to find a way through the fog of uncertainty. All that we can rely upon is the other people who share the uncertainty with us and this requires trust.

Trust develops from an open and honest sharing of information within the organization. When trust does not exist, people share only information that is politically safe to share. Sometimes, information held by employees is deliberately withheld to punish the organization and its managers. This leads to poor problem solving and decision-making that ultimately leads to sub-optimal performance. Furthermore, it leads to cynicism about the values espoused by the organization's senior managers. People generally take little notice of

---

[45] A de Geus, 1997 *The Living Company* . Harvard Business Review, March-April.

what is said – they determine the real values of the organization by how people behave. It is not difficult to imagine that a culture based on blame can form quickly in these circumstances. This develops a set of behaviours that drive people to act in a way that is consistent with bureaucratic management. After all, if people do what they did yesterday and it was politically safe, then it is reasonable to expect that they will do it today and not expose themselves to risk. Blame kills trust, improvement and creativity. It encourages people to adopt inappropriate behaviours by relying only on the tools of mechanistic management in the pursuit of certainty when the tools of extraordinary leadership are necessary.

> **People generally, take little notice of what is said — they determine the real values of the organization by how people behave.**

## Identity and Purpose

It is essential that people within the organization have a clear sense of identity and purpose. When establishing a sense of identity the questions to be asked are, 'What is our history? Who are we? What is unique about us? What is possible for us?'

In discussing organizational change Carr[46] states:

> *It is necessary to go beyond the dichotomous world of rational vs emotional and develop a greater appreciation of how the rational and the emotional can co-exist in a co-dependent fashion. Read through the optic of identity, acts of so-called rationality may simply be an expression of a deeper, albeit unconscious realm, that is, psychodynamics in which emotion and emotionality are significant. It is through the optic of identity that the individual's attachment to the organization and the meaning of behaviour in the midst of change can be described.*

---

[46] Carr, A. (2001) *Understanding emotion and emotionality in a process of change* Journal of Organizational Change Management. Vol 14(5) p421-434.

To have a sense of personal purpose is to become clear about one's own existence within the organization. Finding out the organization's reason for its existence and who and what it is wishing to satisfy helps people to see whether they 'fit' without too much personal accommodation.

We have one client, a CEO, who states that the organization's purpose is to provide challenging and sustainable employment for everyone in the business. Many of those outside the business are horrified that he has not mentioned shareholder wealth etc.

However, what he has done is align the individual's and organization's purpose. Individuals relate to this statement of purpose and choose to be passionately committed to it. This in turn, means they apply the maximum amount of discretionary energy available to sustain their jobs and personal challenge. This is then reflected in the bottom line performance of the business – which is truly extraordinary.

To develop a strong identity and clarity of purpose reduces the need to have rules and structure to govern behaviour. A strong reliance on external controls such as rules and structure is a very clear signal that people in the organization cannot naturally identify with the organizational 'personality'. If they could identify with the organization in this way then, knowing human nature as we do, we have no doubt that they would automatically work in its best interests.

A great deal of time and money is spent by managers on ensuring compliance to the rules and regulations of the organization. At the same time, those being 'managed' spend just as much time avoiding the rules or 'complying' in totally unproductive and sometimes destructive ways. As mentioned before, (employee to customer) "...well, they're the rules and I can't change them. I only work here." We see this like a pressure cooker. Everything rattles along under the surface until one day the pressure blows the lid off. Where we have controls that are externally imposed they will only work in the short term, and only while someone is present to enforce them. After all, we should remember 'imposed rules are owned by someone else and not by me'. Therefore, it seems far more sensible to create an environment where the controls are from within. What we mean here is where the individual or the group chooses to exercise self-control. In these circumstances, flexible responses to deviations in performance can be quickly exercised.

To achieve control through commitment seems infinitely easier and sustainable than through seeking compliance. Self-control in organizations is achievable when people can identify with the business. They behave as if the business is their own. They do not blame the boss, the system or the product when things are not working well. Rather, they look for solutions. It is where people view the business or workplace as an extension of themselves, perhaps a place where they would feel honoured to have their children work. This emotion triggers the release of discretionary energy.

In the case of purpose, people need to feel that the organization is producing a product or providing a service that is valued by the community. Purpose, like identity, is fostered through the collection and sharing of information. Conversely, when rules are imposed, employees do not know why that rule is in place or why they are asked to behave in a particular way or take a particular action. This is true in the health professions. Patient compliance, or lack of, is an issue with which many health care professionals struggle. However, there is a higher rate of 'compliance' when patients actually understand why they have to do what is prescribed. There is even more if they are invited to actively take part in research and the decision making process. Likewise, information and understanding is tantamount to developing both identity and purpose.

There is usually a need to allow people to develop their own purpose. It is interesting when we present this idea to clients they show clear signs of nervousness and apprehension. The big fear is that if we let individuals or work-teams develop their own sense of purpose then the system will become 'chaotic'. 'What happens if their purpose doesn't line up with ours?' is often the question. This example of mechanistic thinking creates the desire for the executive managers to establish the purpose and 'roll it out' through the organization. We do not know of many teams of employees at the value-adding end of the business that can identify deeply with purposes that are distant from their personal ones. Shareholders' returns or the satisfaction of a distant and unknown customer who purchases the product through a distant marketplace such as the London Metals Exchange are hard to take up as causes. Purpose has to be personalised and taken to a level that has meaning for the individual.

It may be useful to refer again to the idea of the strange attractor which, if you remember, acts like a magnet, drawing people in. Leaders can set the boundary (the governing principles that are at the core of the organization's existence) and work out the 'initial conditions', so that they can see how things will look in both the big and small picture. If leaders remain focused on purpose, giving clear direction, they will lead people within the boundary of the initial conditions. No need for hands-on control, remember the mysterious magnetic pull? Responsiveness, flexibility and commitment can all be achieved within the context of the positive development of the organization.

The boundaries set by the strange attractors in the organization will prevent disintegration and total collapse. In fact, it is when managers do what is instinctive (for them) by trying to stabilize and control things that purpose and identity are compromised. When the organization is in turmoil, the search for meaning should be encouraged. The job of leaders is to take a facilitation role, encouraging and supporting existing and new information. It is through the search for meaning we can survive and flourish. Experience has shown us repeatedly, that if teams of people are free to define their own purpose and identity then they feel a greater commitment to the organization, and develop a purpose that is totally congruent with that of the organization's executive. After all, everyone wants to survive.

It is likely that managers will experience regular re-negotiation of boundaries as teams evolve and explore new possibilities. With meaning and purpose in place, employees can be trusted to move freely, with creativity and energy. This is sometimes referred to as 'self-referencing' in the literature. The sharing of information, the working at the relationships level, and the building of identity and purpose are not mutually exclusive activities. As you can imagine, to work on one affects the other two.

## Personal Responsibility

What sort of qualities does the extraordinary leader need to have? Ricardo Semler, owner of Semco and author of 'Maverick'[47] and 'The Seven Day Weekend'[48] gives his version of what real talent is in an organization.


IQ + EQ + SQ **minus EGO**

Intelligence + Emotional Intelligence + Spiritual Intelligence
**minus EGO**


This simple idea captures many of the thoughts and conversations we have had with colleagues we respect. The sort of person we mean here has an over-riding sense of faith in people. S/he has experienced those magical moments when the most truculent, obstructive individual is transformed into the organization's strongest advocate, displays 'the energy of ten men' and starts looking beyond the organization for personal growth and development. What better reward could a leader want than to make it possible for this to happen?

If we look at the last item on Semler's list of qualities, much of the mystery as to why managers manage 'from above' and why they preserve managerial prerogatives almost to their own demise is explained. It is, of course, EGO called in the polite version of the vernacular, 'the big head'. To us, management ego is as much of a consequence as it is a personality trait. We are taught early in life about 'achievers' and how they should be praised. The reward for investing in  management education is position. With the position comes (theoretically) authority and power. 'We have earned this' we can almost hear them saying. The problem comes when managers start to define themselves not by who they are but what they do. At this point, they fit right in to the hierarchical organization.

---

[47] Semler, R. (1993) *Maverick! The Success Story Behind the World's Most Unusual Workplace* New York, Warner Books.
[48] Semler, R. (2003) *The Seven Day Weekend: The Wisdom Revolution, Finding the Work/Life Balance* London, Century (p66).

Hierarchical or bureaucratic organizations are patriarchal in nature. When we start work with a hierarchical organization, Block[49] believes that we agree to four core elements that guide our behaviour. We have used these as labels to share our experiences.

> 1. *Submission to authority*
> 2. *Denial of self- expression*
> 3. *Sacrifice for unnamed future rewards*
> 4. *Belief that the above are just.*

## 1. Submission to Authority

Everyone in the organization reports to someone and the first thing we are told when we join is who that person is. A foundation of most organizations is that the bureaucratic lines of power need to be clear and understood. Because those lines of power run down the organization, we accept that control of our work and behaviour is in the hands of those above. The power relationship remains unquestioned with the key element being 'submission'. When we submit to the authority of others, we accept that the most trustworthy source of knowledge does not exist within us but exists beyond ourselves. As a consequence, we experience a feeling of dependency that encourages us to seek approval. The benefit of submitting to the authority of those above is the release from personal responsibility. It provides us with the ultimate excuse when something goes wrong – its not our fault, it is the boss who is at fault. After all, the boss 'owns' the system in which we operate. Blame is likely to become our normal response.

This dependency on the power of those above creates a feeling of helplessness in those without power. Managers, on the one hand, take comfort in the fact that there are people under their control. This gives them the illusion of power and influence and the feeling that they fulfil a vital role in the organization.

The people who work for them take comfort in the fact that when things go wrong, it is not their fault. They do not have to take ultimate responsibility. The price that they pay for this comfort is a feeling of 'helplessness'.

---

[49] Block, P. (1987) The empowered manager: Positive political skills at work in San Francisco, Jossey-Bass.

But the illusion is with the issue of power and control and who really has it. Beattie[50] talks about the definition of co-dependency (not to be confused with interdependency).

> *A co-dependent is one who has let another person's behaviour affect him or her, and who is obsessed with controlling that person's behaviour.*

Beattie sites another definition by Robert Stubby[51] :

> *An emotional, psychological and behavioural condition that develops as a result of an individual's prolonged exposure to and practice of, a set of oppressive rules – rules which prevent the open expression of feeling as well as the direct discussion of personal and interpersonal problems.*

Now, you might say, 'but the managers are the ones controlling.' Yes, in an illusionary sense, but looking back to our story about the accidental shutdown of the plant – who was really controlling (by lack of information)? Management or the plant operator? A lot of research has been conducted on co-dependency, mainly in the area of personal relationships. The following lists just some of the identifiable behaviours of co-dependency: victim behaviour, low self-worth, repression, obsession, control, denial, dependency, poor communication, lack of trust, anger, blame, manipulation, fear, withholding information by covering up, helplessness, and not saying what is truly meant. Sound familiar? One has to wonder about the long-term effect of mechanistic organizations – the effect certainly doesn't promote self-responsibility or a climate that demands that one stretch oneself to full potential or realisation.

With this in mind, let's continue with Block's points.

## 2. Denial of Self-Expression

People in mechanistic organizations believe that it is necessary to censor what they say. In fact, it is associated with the choice to

---

[50] Beattie, M. (1992). *Codependent No More* Minnesota. Hazelton.
[51] Cited in Beattie, M. (1992). *Codependent No More* Minnesota, Hazelton.

submit to the power that runs down the organization. People are encouraged to be rational, logical and get on with the task at hand. There is no room for any conversation about feelings and beliefs.

When we avoid conversations about feelings we attack the integrity of the organization. After all, feelings generate the willingness or the discretionary energy that is essential to achieving a high performing organization. Because we care deeply about what happens at work, in both task and relationship terms, we are going to have strong feelings about the workplace. To deny the expression of those feelings is costly to both the individual and the organization.

Managers usually look for ways to motivate the people working for them. The source of all energy, passion, motivation and the internal desire to produce quality work is our feelings about what we are doing. It has little to do with the rational business processes that we embrace. The inability to express our feelings and aspirations, together with the need to submit to authority, dampens our willingness and passion. It deprives the organization of our discretionary energy. In other words, if we don't address feeling, we can't expect discretionary energy. This is about building wealth by paying attention to the intangible assets of the organization.

The fear we have, however, is that if we encourage talk about feelings somehow, the organization's work will be compromised. We fear people will do their own thing, and we shall be out of control. This fear of losing control leads us to feel comfortable with a relationship that does not tolerate behaviour or thoughts which are outside the mainstream, even if that wish for control is at the expense of performance. And so often, we see examples of performance being compromised for the sake of control.

### 3. Sacrifice for Unnamed Future Rewards

The third psychological agreement we have with our organization is to make sacrifices. Sacrifices involve doing something that does not make sense to those asked to make them, or do something they would not normally do. Sacrifices incur an obligation. That is, in return for the sacrifice, there is the promise of a future reward.

Where making sacrifices is a basic element of our relationship with the organization, there is a hidden price to pay. We see this played out so often in the industrial relations area where there is a desire for 'payback' for the sacrifices made.

Many people join large organizations out of a wish for safety, security and a comfortable future. There was a time when organizations could promise that sort of future, but that time has passed.

The syndrome of major retrenchments, even in government organizations, signals the end of this psychological contract. The contract has been violated because we can no longer promise people that if they work hard, sacrifice and commit themselves to the organization, there will always be a secure future for them. To build an organization based on people sacrificing for future gain is indeed, a tenuous proposition.

## 4. A Belief That the Above are Just

When we believe that submission to authority, practicing self-censorship and making sacrifices are just and good for us and the organization, they will be exercised by us. However, these three elements create dependency. To believe that they are good for the organization is to believe that dependency is good business and simply put, continues to promote this type of behaviour. To believe otherwise raises the fear that we will lose control and drift into a state of anarchy. The strongest wish of a mechanistic organization is to maintain control at all costs.

There is a widespread belief in external power to maintain order. It is believed that, if no strong lines of power come from above and outside the individual, we would find the organization heading for disintegration. This belief suggests that if people are left to their own instincts and authority, they will somehow act in ways that run counter to the organization. If that is the case, then we have a pessimistic view that people do not wish to act responsibly. As a result of that view, we believe that external authority must be constantly applied to keep employees focused on the organization's goals. There is a belief here that people are not able to exercise adequate self-control. Such beliefs fly in the face of experience and the theory of complex adaptive systems[52] (which is where we find many of the characteristics of chaos and complexity mentioned earlier).

The more irresponsible the behaviour we see, the more tightly we control, and the more we believe that external control is essential to achieve the organization's purpose. In a way this is counter to arguments supporting the objective of 'quality at the source' presented by Total Quality Management models.

High levels of external control, however, allow people the opportunity to avoid taking responsibility. Further to this, traditional managers believe that if we want clear structure, if we want clarity and simplicity of goals and purpose with little disagreement, then the easiest way to achieve this is through autocratic high command and control behaviour.

We have conditioned people to operate in highly structured environments, so when some of the structure is taken away to give the organization flexibility to respond to its customers' needs, we have found that one can expect a period when people may test how much authority they have. They may act in their own interests, some of which will not be in the best interests of the organization (this is where the values approach provides sound guidelines). Therefore, one could conclude that external controls are necessary. However, what we are ignoring is that unpredictable events that are not in the best interests of the organization also take place in highly controlled structures. High-control, top-down structures create their own resistance. We are going to lose control no matter what kind of external control structure we create.

In fact, the actual control the manager believes he has is a fantasy. A manager believes that s/he has every right to tell people what to do, but in reality people decide whether they are going to comply or not.

The alternative is to adopt the belief that the ultimate authority for our actions comes from within. People are responsible for all of their

---

[52] Waldrop, M. M. (1992) *Complexity: The Emerging Science at the Edge of Order and Chaos* London, Viking.

actions despite what is happening in the culture and the environment in which they operate. Ultimately people make their own choices and the focus of control for their actions is internal.

The paradox is that our efforts at maintaining control, maintaining authority, and denying self-expression fuels the drive for other people to fight against what we are trying to control. It prevents people from doing what is in the best interests of the organization and its customers. When people are allowed to express their feelings and be authentic, performance increases.

In many mechanistic organizations, the wish to maintain control is much stronger than the wish to improve performance. In the workplace, for example, we find that there are some who prefer and choose to maintain victim mentality rather than be self-responsible. One of the reasons for this could be the development of 'learned helplessness'[53]. What prevents them from shifting is the lack of positive experience. However, as mentioned earlier, a pessimistic view will influence perception, so it becomes a circular process with no way out. In extreme cases where mentoring doesn't work, it may be necessary for a professional to intervene using for example 'fixed role therapy'[54]. This is a method based on personal construct theory which allows the person to 'experience' new ways of being, and in doing so, gains positive results which refute old beliefs. If a person continues to deliberately breach the values agreement, then the organization needs to exercise agreed consequences. This should be made clear when developing the values in the first instance.

> **In many mechanistic organizations, the wish to maintain control is much stronger than the wish to improve performance.**

---

[53] Seligman, M. (1993) *Learned Optimism* . New York, Random House
[54] Brophy, S. & Epting, F. (1996). *Mentoring Employees: A Role for Personal Construct Psychology* (In *Personal Construct Theory – a Psychology for the Future*. Eds. Walker, B.M., Costigan, , J.,Viney L.L & Warren. , B. Australian Psychological Society (p *239-252*).

If managers have to choose between 'giving up control' for the sake of higher performance, and maintaining control knowing performance will be inhibited, in most cases they will choose control. This often causes tension between what is said i.e. 'we want performance', and the actions that are focused on control, usually at the expense of performance.

This reinforces peoples' belief that their survival is dependent on the attitude and approval of their boss. It reinforces their belief that their performance is outside their control. The result is an organization riddled with negative political behaviour, blame and victim mentality.

This relationship satisfies both parties - the managers who want control and the subordinates who want to avoid responsibility - but does nothing to improve performance.

When an organization is far from certainty and far from agreement, the hierarchical relationship is unable to deliver the performance sought from the organization. No longer can people rely on their bosses to provide direction and make decisions. People must weigh up the situation with which they are confronted and turn their judgment into action. Sooner or later we must realize that there is nothing to wait for and that our dependency on those above is not serving us or the organization well at all. We must choose to act whilst recognizing the interdependent nature of our actions. The ability to exercise judgment is mandatory when practicing personal responsibility

Our goal is to have all members believe and act as they would if it was their own organization, and to take personal responsibility for how it operates. This begins to happen when we develop extraordinary leadership, which is based on the belief that the most trustworthy source of authority comes from within us. The primary task of leadership is to help people trust their own instincts and judgments. It is about encouraging people to take responsibility for the success of the organization. People do that bit extra that achieves performance because they want to, not because they have to.

Extraordinary leadership also requires us to define success in terms of contribution and service rather than promotion within the organization.

What we need to offer as rewards along with advancement and pay are jobs that have meaning with the opportunity to learn and create something special and the chance to grow through our efforts. Can you possibly imagine what would happen if the guidelines for employment were based on these values? The primary focus needs to be on the intangible rewards for everyone in the organization.

We need to be genuine, which encourages us to be direct and definite. If we have a strong identity with our organization, then we will feel empowered to act on our own values. This means letting people know where they stand. They need to know the consequences of violating shared values. They need to be encouraged to share information and control, and take reasonable risks. Although it makes sense, it takes courage.

Allowing people more autonomy reduces the need to give so much attention and power to those above us. It reduces the fear of being 'shot' and demands that we take responsibility for our actions. Furthermore, we need to talk freely and openly about our thoughts, feelings, beliefs and dreams within the workplace and make strong personal commitments. We need to trust ourselves.

A colleague and friend, William Conway, recently suggested in his newsletter that

> The idea of 'responsibility' asserts that individually we say we are accountable for our actions - and we are willing to take internal control of our attitudes, emotions and reactions. We govern ourselves, knowing that the baser side of our natures is only too willing to place the blame of circumstances on others. However as people begin to develop the victim's mentality, the idea of responsibility quickly degrades into something called 'obligation.' This is where EXTERNAL controls are placed on us, and we obey laws and social conventions because we 'have to'. Incidental to this is the idea of disciplinary action if we don't!

> What I believe we've witnessed in the last 50 years is a further step away from personal responsibility; into a self-centred philosophy of 'MY RIGHTS'! The 'rights' movement strongly suggests the highest ideal is 'what's good for me'.

*Volunteerism and service fly in the face of this philosophy, in my opinion. Service focuses on what's good for the fellow down the street. Thus, the confrontation between these opposing philosophies is inevitable, and can be clearly seen in the preponderance of litigation in our courts. Burglars sue home-owners for not providing adequate safety systems when they cut themselves on skylights in the normal conduct of their 'vocations'.*

*Ayn Rand was wrong - there is no 'virtue in selfishness'. Recovering communities of care where we look after one another without the threat of litigation is, I believe, a worthy objective. But it's not a short-term goal. It will require a return to personal responsibility. It will require maturity.[55]*

It also requires courage.

## Customer Focus

Perhaps one of the few pieces of certainty for organizations is that they need to know and meet their customers' needs. No one would argue that failure to do so results in organizational death.

At times there is considerable tension in meeting the customers' needs. The tension arises from the competing objectives of the organization and its customers. On the one hand, customers demand flexible approaches to the production and delivery of goods and services. On the other hand, organizations aim to achieve certainty and predictability to deliver efficiencies. Here we have paradox again. Many organizations put processes in place to meet their own goals rather than meet those of their customers.

There are many examples of tension in every day life. For example, in the banking industry, bank employees are constantly confronted with unusual requests from customers.

The usual response is that it can't be done because it is outside the rules. People from the manufacturing sector tell the same story.

---

[55] Conway. W W. (2004) Unpublished email, *E-clips*, at wvecon@bigpond.com.au

Small to medium sized customers, who themselves operate in an unpredictable world, have to learn to respond flexibly and to adapt. Those small to medium organizations often deal with large multi-national suppliers of product or service who are interested in maintaining long inflexible production runs to meet their cost objectives – the result is tension.

For employees, the question is, 'Do I serve my customers or do I serve my organizational masters?' Generally, the response is to serve the organizational masters since it is the organization that provides the short-term needs of safety and security. However, serving the organizational objectives at the expense of the customers, leads to a slow but inevitable death for the organisation, with the consequent impact on the employees.

> ## 'Do I serve my customers or do I serve my organizational masters?'

It is often argued that in looking after customers, you are also looking after the organization. Whilst agreeing with this proposition, it is difficult to ask people to accept short-term pain and disruption for the long-term benefit of the organization. The organisation needs to promote a genuine customer focus and behave in a way that is congruent with the messages delivered.

People at all levels need to have close relationships and regular contact with customers and not restrict that contact to the marketing arm or the senior managers of the organization. Every organization needs to maximize its capacity to collect information and intelligence and to build long-term sustainable partnerships with customers.

It is probably wise and timely to drop the idea of customers and suppliers since there is a mythology and history built around such relationships. It is usually associated with power running in one direction only, unless the supplier is in a monopoly situation.

We think that the term 'partnership' expresses more clearly the type of relationships that are necessary for the survival of modern organizations. It becomes a relationship built on trust and mutual benefit.

---

**The term "partnership" expresses more clearly the type of relationships that are necessary for the survival of modern organizations.**

---

**Points to ponder**

Thinking about the intangible assets of the organization, which of the ideas and concepts in both part one and part two of this chapter has the most potential to grow the wealth of the organization?

If you were in the lift with the CEO or Chairman, and you had a one minute journey to the top floor, how would you explain the ideas you have chosen above in a simple yet persuasive way?

We have now worked through the conceptual model of Extraordinary Leadership and later in Chapter 8 we will review these attributes once again to refresh your memory.

We are sure that by now you might be asking, "So how do we put those ideas into practice?". The next chapter explains how that journey might begin – through the Extraordinary Leadership Workshop. Perhaps it is not the only way to begin, since in leading organisations into extraordinary performance, there are many ways available, but it is a way that has proved successful for us and many others.

This is followed by the powerful tool known as PATOP. It is a tool that can be used to support the performance initiatives on a daily basis.

We then go on to explore our view of why organizations have reached the position that they often find themselves in and some reasons for resistance to those ideas espoused by the model of Extraordinary Leadership.

Chapter 9 looks at the shackles placed on us by the bureaucratic nature of organizations.

# Notes

# EXTRAORDINARY LEADERSHIP WORKSHOP

## The Workshop

The Extraordinary Leadership Workshop lies at the heart of this book. The theories, concepts and ideas we have presented throughout the book all have some connection with the workshop. Over the years, approximately 5,000 employees from various companies have experienced the workshop. As we said in the introduction to the book, it is difficult to convey the ambience at the beginning of the workshop week with that at the closing session. The change is most apparent in the ways that participants, managers, workers, leaders, (all relieved of their official status for the week) express thoughts and feelings about the quality of life at work. Possibilities have opened up and some of these in the most restricting of circumstances. Networks form, not for one or two week afterwards, as we tend to experience, but as lasting relationships where support can be asked for and automatically received. In fact in one organization, there is a healthy email network that operates outside of the formal system (Stacey would call this the shadow system) and where the spirit of the workshop is kept alive.

## Complex Adaptive Systems - a Memory Jog

Before we go on to describe the workshop, we need just to remind the reader of the essence of complex adaptive systems so that you can appreciate the basis for the thinking underpinning many of the workshop decisions such as no agendas, letting communities happen naturally, inserting some disturbance into the workshop and challenging the value of unquestioning compliance with rules. The theory, which you met in chapter four, is, of course, complex adaptive systems theory.

The essence of the theory of complex adaptive systems lies in its non-linear, adaptive, self-organizing qualities. It sits well within a turbulent context and we propose that much of life today fits into that category. Let's look at this in a little more detail. The pace of work is faster than ever, and the expectations of 'smarts' as a way to beat the productivity clock have risen too. Because scientism and mechanistic management still loom large in organizations, managers are expected to know more about technology, and they have to keep abreast of new rules and regulations too. Working life is more complex as risk management and quality audits criss-cross with each other and with other administrative processes. Information overload is on the increase and managers have email, i-mail, hard mail and person-mail. Home life for many people is more turbulent than peaceful with education being more competitive, jobs less secure, and expectations higher, not to mention the overload on the psyche of the constant bombardment of consumer messages. There are some positive messages within the turbulent context, but not for those who seek order, predictability, familiarity and the security that comes with habit. In fact traditional workplaces are probably the only places that still put considerable effort into emulating a calm and regulated existence.

Youngblood[56] captures the sort of qualities embedded in the workshop design. Organizations are seen as wholes, as opposed to being frag-mented into work teams or departments. Due to the constant interaction and production of new ways to see and share things, the wholes are always greater than the sum of their parts. As people interact and veer off in their conversations, things get re-interpreted and re-invented, taking the conversations and practices far from the comfortable start-ing point that we call equilibrium. The more people create new ways of doing things (and in the doing, discard the old) the more stable struc-tures and the balance they produce get in the way. By knocking things out of balance, effort has to be put into renewal and hopefully in different forms. As people are liberated from formal language, formal meetings, traditional roles, they find new ways of working that can, to the outside observer, be confusing. That is because often there is no direct 'this leads to that' and 'if we do this, then we know what will happen'.

Things might happen in roundabout ways and there is always room for surprises. In fact they are mandatory in the complex adaptive systems environment. There is more interconnectivity and autonomy

[56] Youngblood, M. (1997) *Life at the Edge of Chaos: Creating the Quantum Organization*, Richardson, Texas, Perceval Publishing.

than straight line connections and compliance and, one of the reasons why predictability is so difficult is that there is what we might call an ecological web of relationships which is constantly changing and adapting to new or re-constructed information coming in. As a basic condition, the complex adaptive system needs to be freed from certainty, predictability, linear thinking and an over-reliance on rational thinking. David set the workshop up, as far as possible, as a self-organizing system. Of course, like complex adaptive systems, the workshop had its initial conditions – clear objectives, agreed values and negotiable and non-negotiable boundaries. Behaviours, opinions, arguments, information were allowed to emerge.

There was ample room for spontaneity and trial and error. Opportunities for 'real', not always detectable, learning abounded due to the action-learning framework (described below). Negative as well as positive feedback loops were designed into the workshop so that the power of feedback could be felt naturally. Diversity of opinion and a strong sense of voluntarism were allowed scope. Creativity (especially around rules and traditions) was encouraged through a discovery and discussion approach. The workshop was designed so that surprises were a feature and disturbance was factored somewhere into the day. Participants became very sensitive to non-verbal information and in response to this, for example, when David was calling the group together he kept speeding up the musical signal and walk became run.

Every one of the qualities we mention above has been designed either into the thinking or the practice of the workshop. This makes it so hard to describe it in traditional terms. So what we decided to do was to leave this task to past participants. Kathrine recently interviewed some of the program participants of the leadership workshops. She was intrigued at the way people referred to the week's experience as 'IT'. The following, she tells us, is quite representative of many of the conversations she held.

> 'IT' is the feeling … the change … a euphoria and enlightenment … being true to yourself …inner acceptance …switched a light inside my head …the whole course …ability to speak to people about what you truly feel, not what you think they would want to hear to make them happy …coming to terms with yourself and the way

*you interact with people ....confidence in myself to (say) exactly what I'm thinking ...a realization ...it gave me the strength to make the right decisions ...from here (pointing to heart) not from here (head) ...you can't call it a word, you can't call it anything, that's why I just call it 'IT'. You learn 'IT' while you're there ...'*

In the following extract, the participant makes an interesting observation that there are things he just did without thinking. Over time, (and we would say that in living with too many formal structures and norms) not only had people become inhibited but they seemed not to notice that this was happening.

*'It's hard to explain without actually doing 'IT', but the easiest thing would be ... you learn something there that you've always known, but through work, relationships with people, experience in life, whatever, it gets pushed aside ... When you're a kid you just do that, but as you get older you start to learn you can't say what you feel all the time ...you become inhibited. You're restricted because you start to consider others ...what you're actually doing is conforming to society, and what David teaches you at the course is that you DON'T HAVE TO CONFORM ... when the 'light' flicked on, I realised that 'IT' was something that I'd always known, but you just couldn't use 'IT' as you get older and now he's teaching you how to use 'IT', or to realise that you've still got that ability, but also to use 'IT' properly.'*

The extraordinary leadership workshop story began in the mid-nineties. David was commissioned by a large global steel manufacturer to develop a workshop that would change the culture of one of the plants within the steel works. The key drivers for the cultural change were the need to improve the safety performance through the creation of a culture of care and, to improve the plant's productivity. The Workshop aimed to give participants an experience of leadership and teamwork that encouraged a strong personal commitment to making a positive difference in their organizations. It was built using an action-learning model.

Action learning is a process in which a group of people come together to help each other learn from their experience. The participants typically came from different situations, where each of them was involved in different activities and faced individual problems within one organization. It is usual for the team to consist of people with a common task or problem. To us, action learning is a process by which change and understanding need to happen at the same time. It is usually described as cyclic, with action and critical reflection taking place in turn. The reflection is used to review the previous action and plan the next one. Mike Pedler[57], building on the work of Reg Revans[58] shares ideas that echo the way we see learning and change. 'Here is an acid test: you can tell whether this is Action Learning or not by whether people are exercising moral imagination, by how often they question their own and each others' actions and by how much they strive towards integrity for themselves and their colleagues ... the process of 'outer' (actions) and 'inner' (learnings) is one which questions of value interact with the practical matters of managing'. To take this route is not an easy one because it is like leaving the safety of a calm stream and suddenly hitting rocks and shoals. As soon as values and any moral element come into learning situations, courage and emotional competence become essential qualities of the facilitator. One of the challenges in such a workshop is to be willing to be directed by the workshop team members.

**The Beginning – What No Agenda?**

So where do we start? Careful attention is paid to the physical layout of the workshop. Very few of the 'props' that participants and facilitators alike lean on are there. To begin with, there are no tables on which the participants can lean or psychologically hide behind. Second, the chairs are placed in a circle to encourage communication. Perhaps it is similar to the traditional campfire where people sit around a cental point (the fire) and tell stories.

The fact that there is no published agenda is emphasised during the introduction. Participants are told, however, that *as facilitators* we have a very clear overall mission to meet their needs. We find it difficult to publish an agenda and at the same time to invite participants to shape the week to ensure that their own needs are

[57] Pedler, M. (1991) *Action Learning in Practice* Aldershot, Hants, Gower (p35).
[58] Revans, R. W. (1983) *The ABC of Action Learning* Bromley, Chartwell-Bratt.

met. To some extent, the publication of an agenda in these types of workshops could be seen as an arrogant statement because the workshop facilitators are effectively saying that they know what the participants need. Bang goes the certainty and also the agreement from this diverse group about what the needs might be.

Of course, that does not trouble us as much as it troubles participants, who mostly want to slot in to whatever structure is presented. Stimulating uncertainty is the most important reason for not publishing an agenda. Uncertainty, we believe, is where most of the real world lives. As the week develops, the claims of certainty held on to by participants soon take on a mythical air. Even though at the beginning, people want and expect a map or a plan, it becomes clear that uncertainty is natural, has to be lived through, and is rich in possibilities for learning. The workshop creates an environment where actions and learning are developed from the experiences of the week. As the reader can imagine, this is not what is normally expected at the beginning of a workshop on leadership and change.

It is this uncertainty and the inability of participants to seek comfort in the workshop leaders or a map or plan that brings people together. Faced with situations that are far from certain and far from agreement as far as participants are concerned, they have to learn how to deal with the many unexpected circumstances that they are confronted with throughout the week. These circumstances provide the basis for developing and experiencing trust among the participants. After all, they only have each other on whom to rely.

Another important feature of the workshops is that the participants must discover for themselves what they believe is useful for them from a broad range of learning events. As we have said, participants are not given a plan for the week. A journey of discovery rather than one of completion presents itself. As people discover for themselves what the workshop is about for them, they are given an opportunity to make sense of it through the lens of their personal experiences and aspirations.

**The First Day**

The first day is devoted to developing the workshop community. In keeping with what we explained earlier, this is largely done by the participants (not the least in the bar later – to which teetotallers are also invited. Thanks from Alma to the 'fine and dandy' group). The sharing of information is a key feature and it, in turn, helps develop relationships. From those relationships a sense of identity starts to emerge. Time and time again, we have seen that as participants do things together, and they certainly do that from day one, identity forms. There is a value underlying the workshop and this is presented for the participants to make of, as they will. The value is expressed through a simple but powerful model of performance. That is, *performance* is a function of having a clear *direction* and, a *willingness* to pursue that direction with passion and energy. This can be represented by the formula Performance (P) = Direction (D) + Willingness (W) and participants are told that the workshop focuses on ways to generate willingness (or discretionary energy), more than on providing clarity of direction. Simulating a rational, systematic process of direction setting would, we think, validate the 'control from above' approach that we have talked about so much in earlier chapters.

So apart from the values, do we go in blind, with no tools and framework? No. There are certain tools, both knowledge and skills-based that fit in well with the uncertainty and control-from-within nature of the workshop. The first we have described already and this is action learning, developed by the famous Reg Revans[59] as a device to bring fresh thinking and learning to diverse groups and individuals. The engineering of the workshop is underpinned by Kolb's[60] learning cycle. First participants 'do' things together. This is the experience. Then they are encouraged to learn through the process of *reflection*. They then have a 'talk time' with a partner every day and problems and issues are tried out, mulled over and generally tried on for size.

### As the Week Develops

We break our story here to share with you a gift from a past workshop participant.

---

[59] Revans, R. W. (1983) *The ABC of Action Learning* Bromley, Chartwell-Bratt.
[60] Kolb, D. Rubin, I. and McIntyre, J. (1979) Organizational Psychology, 3rd Ed Englewood Cliffs, New Jersey. Prentice Hall

### Along The Path

*This is my commitment to Work Place Change and the people with whom I live and work.*

*I promise to walk down this path we are on, taking one step at a time. Some big, some small, some confidently and some hesitantly.*

*Most of the time we will walk together. Sometimes I may lead and sometimes I will follow. Sometimes I may feel alone and sometimes I may feel crowded.*

*When confronted by sudden or unexpected obstacles, I will probably stop and consider my options. I may even take a step back, just for security. I hope that I will not turn and run.*

*Along the way I may stumble at some point where the path is uneven, if I do there are four possible outcomes:*

*1. I may fall. Scratched, battered and maybe even broken I may turn around and limp home to recover.*

*2. I may fall, and if not too damaged, I may get up and continue on the path. But human kinetics being what they are, as I get up I will probably find myself one step further along the path.*

*3. I may not fall, but save myself from any damage, other than a bent ego, by taking one quick step forward to get back onto the even path.*

*4. Or, as has been reinforced to me by my participation in the Work Place Change session, there may be someone there to catch me and help me back onto the even path.*

*I promise to try to keep walking down this path with all of you, one step at a time.*

### Chris Hackett

In the action learning spirit, workshop members go into small teams. They are asked to work on a project to improve the performance, safety and satisfaction of the workplace. This in a way, provides a 'purpose' element of the week where there is a genuine problem to be solved. The project enables the participants to link the various learning throughout the week along a common thread and simultaneously consider the application of the workshop learning to their individual workplaces. They are encouraged to consider ways that they can make a positive difference in their workplaces. At times, heralded by rousing music, the community meets to share whatever is going on.

Some interesting things happen in workshop teams that relate directly to the cautions we gave earlier about seeking certainty and control. The teams invariably begin by gathering the time honoured materials needed to 'present' to others. Newsprint, whiteboards, and sheets of notes are produced so that 'progress can be seen'. What progress, we ask them? Is it possible to see a learning system develop? Does it mean that by making a presentation, some closure has been reached? As you were there and the project is for yourselves, what purpose does the 'report' serve?

One comment we make is that it is so much harder to challenge, demolish and/or contradict items that once may have been taken on a tangible form. This leads to the question of just when do things need to be formally reported? What role does habit play in the ways we almost automatically record meetings? Take the topic of minutes. Almost all meetings have as the first item on the agenda 'confirmation of past minutes'. This is so that we can be 'certain' and 'have agreement' with what was said. Was what was said, what was meant we sometimes ask? And if not, what might have been the barriers to open and honest communication? What would we do in our meetings if we were liberated from the format and followed one that reflected complex adaptive systems, CAS?

We make this happen in the program. Interspersed throughout the week are some activities that cause people to confront and to be confronted. One particular activity somewhat resembles the 'prisoners dilemma' that management developers sometimes use, where prisoners who are put in separate cells can be rewarded or otherwise for either supporting each other or 'turning each other in'. A situation is set up so that two teams, working individually, have the opportunity to a) cooperate or compete b) be honest or bend the truth. As you can see, the permutations are many. The honesty element puts some of the 'moral imagination' in that Mike Pedler[61] talks about in action learning. At no time does one team know what the other is doing. Listening in on the teams, we hear problems such as 'do we shaft them or not'? 'What do we want to do, be nice or win the game?' (It is those who say immediately that they went all out to win the game that carry that reflection in their behaviour to the closing session). There is, of course no right answer in such a program as the workshop and when the teams come together to hear what each has done, it is easy to see individuals struggling with their personal dilemmas. They are also, through such events, brought face to face with paradox, contradiction and 'if-then' thinking. Some issues that are part of the informal life of organizations but not so much in task-oriented environments involve the 'currency' of relationship maintenance. We can report from the many closing sessions of the workshops that, once invited to combine relational needs with task needs, there is an added vibrancy to tackling practical tasks.

In a nutshell, there is a certain amount of chaos factored into the week's activities. We found in practice what writers say in theory, that is, from chaos comes new order. Out of the chaos of the week, comes a new order – a new way of viewing organizational behaviour and systems. This new view slowly develops as participants experience the many opportunities and dilemmas incorporated into the workshop. For many, it is on days three and four that new possibilities emerge. Why so late? This is because, for some, there is a comfort zone of compliance and personal withdrawal so strong that to release them brings great apprehension. Once it is released and personal growth and identity are free to develop then there is a transformation amazing to see. 'IT' – the transformation - has happened and for many there will be no going back. The discovery of new possibilities or the surprise that comes from that act of discovery is what helps develop energy and willingness among the participants.

---

[61] Pedler, M. (1991) *Action Learning in Practice* Aldershot, Hants, Gower.

## Observations and Learning

### Values, Feelings and Trust

It is always interesting to observe the reaction of participants to the first day's activities. Early in the day participants are divided into four teams that participate in a simulation where each team is obliged to maximise the profits available in the market place. The teams can only maximise profits by co-operating with one another. Competing with each other guarantees sub-optimal outcomes for the market place as a whole and leads to unsustainable outcomes. Often people begin the exercise without becoming clear about its purpose and they usually fail to explore the various strategies available to them. In addition, the participants often fail to challenge the assumptions that they have made about the purpose and the behaviour of others.

How often do we, in our busy organizations, stop to clarify the objective that we are pursuing, explore the various possibilities for completing tasks and fail to check the validity of the assumptions made? On the latter point, we often behave and make decisions on the basis that our assumptions are unquestioningly valid. On the other two points, we may at times, clarify the objective handed down but how often do we go into exploration of possibilities, especially when it is expected that we will 'follow procedure'.

When participants' values are violated, the feelings aroused are negative towards the perpetrators of the violation. These feelings are often strong and are held for a number of days. It is clear therefore, that to violate values, even in minor ways, causes long lasting negativity on the part of the person affected. Unlike in many organizations, the workshop is a place where such things are shared, mulled over and reflected upon. Participants talk about 'walking a mile in the others' shoes'. There is a clear metaphor for events that may occur in organizations. Participants clearly understand the consequences of 'violations', such as the all-important breakdown of trust.

Because of the liberating atmosphere in the workshop people do not have to act out politically or boss-pleasing behaviours. As people are freed up, there may well be a point in the workshop where the beliefs of many of the participants are violated. The violated ones are understandably volatile and emotional. Participants learn first hand the futility of being told to be rational and logical under those circumstances. David tells a story of one participant who found David's role-play behaviour unacceptable and picked him up and pinned him to the wall of the conference room to prevent the continuation of that behaviour. When Alma was interviewing people at that particular workplace recently to do with relationship risks, the story had passed into organizational lore. It was quite surprising to see that (apart from being very tall and strong) the individual was a quiet, reflective and caring man. How powerful and natural the emotions must have been for him to react in such a way. We propose to you that organizations would rather apply rational solutions ('make the people see sense') than become engaged in a supportive way with the emotional undercurrents that are often behind 'deviant' behaviour.

**Tension**

Throughout the week, constant tension exists. This is partly caused by the uncertainty about what happens next, since there is no published agenda and the facilitators do not volunteer such information.

The second source of tension is caused by wildly fluctuating emotions. On a particular day it is not uncommon to begin with an exercise that challenges the personal space and beliefs that people hold. Shortly afterwards, the participants experience sadness and disappointment followed by humour, discovery and joy. Next they may experience shock at behaviour that violates their values and beliefs and then be expected to shift to a totally rational exercise. Those events simulate the normal day-to-day life within organizations where many participants will go back to a work environment that clearly acts in ways contrary to the positive experiences of the week.

Out of the workshop develops a new 'footprint' for beliefs, attitudes and behaviours. People discover that certainty within human systems is a fantasy. It was once suggested by a colleague, that 'order is the dream of man and chaos is the law of nature'. There is a tension between our deepest desire for order, predictability and certainty and the reality of organizations existing at the edge of chaos where they are obviously far from certainty. This source of tension is constantly addressed throughout the workshop.

The moment of tension for each individual is a special point in the workshop and it occurs at different points for each individual. It is the point where interaction with others releases creativity and new insights in each participant. When the magic of the moment of tension works, people are able to achieve unimaginable results. Together with the other participants, each individual is able to lift the performance of everyone involved. However, at the moment of tension, results may be sporadic and unpredictable and leaders of organizations must be prepared to live with that outcome.

Unmanaged tension can be detrimental. Tension that is pushed underground causes negative political behaviour to emerge, often in the form of power plays. When leaders ignore the tension and live in the fantasy that it does not exist, they are effectively making the organization leaderless. Leaderless organizations expose themselves to the risk of becoming aligned to those forces acting upon them and within them. It is possible for groups such as trade unions to have a disproportionate influence on the activities of the organization or for people to align themselves closely to their professional body rather that the employing organization.

### Sustainability and Support from Organizations

The inevitable question is 'Can the passion be maintained?' The answer is yes and no. Taking the 'no', it is most unlikely that the same level of excitement and passion can be sustained for long periods when participants return to work. The participants have changed but the work place, in general, changes at a much slower rate. This is not to say that the energy is totally lost, rather it has become somewhat overwhelmed by the normal routines and pressures in the workplace.

On the 'yes' side, the energy and commitment is usually not lost. It is surprising that with very little follow-up people are quickly able to revisit the experiences of the workshop and a renewed enthusiasm becomes obvious.

On some occasions, participants return to a rather hostile workplace and they find it difficult to honour their personal commitments in those circumstances. A safe strategy for those participants is to discount or deny the workshop experience. There is a double loss here. The first is that choosing a strategy of denial often drags the participants into feeling like victims of the organization's hierarchical behaviour. The second is that people in this position not only discount the workshop, but they disconnect with the organization. At a deep level they become angry and frustrated with the organization and its management.

Participants have learned to challenge the command and control mindset of the organization and to explore what has to be done to capitalise on the investment made in employees through the workshops. In cases where senior managers did not understand how complex adaptive organizations work, the workshops create considerable internal tension due to the contradictory behaviour of those who encouraged people to participate in the workshops. The contradictory behaviour is further aggravated when people act in ways that are different to what they espouse.

There have also been examples of organizations where abdication of responsibility was the result of a lack of understanding of complex adaptive systems. In these circumstances, managers just stepped away from taking responsibility for leadership since they usually only had one model of behaviour – command and control. In their minds, the only alternative was to do nothing. The result of abdication by management was confusion and poor performance. Often people become frustrated by the lack of consequences for positive and negative outcomes particularly when dysfunctional and un-productive behaviour is ignored. Whilst people do not generally want control placed on them, they do want the organization to show leadership and direction, and to allow people to choose internal control in the pursuit of shared goals. The pursuit of organizational goals needs to be achieved in a way that is consistent with the expressed shared values of the organization.

The workshop is most successful where the organization's leadership has developed a deep understanding of complex adaptive systems and provided systems and behaviour to support the idea that the behaviour of individuals gets magnified through the system. It becomes possible to challenge each individual to make a difference in everything that they do – even the small things. Such organizations accept that whilst planning is necessary, responsiveness is valued more than prediction. Those organizations that see themselves as complex adaptive systems view prediction as a fantasy – an ideal or a dream. It is recognised that we would all feel a lot better if there was certainty about the future, but this is not the normal experience of humans. If it were the normal experience of organizations, prediction would be a more useful endeavour.

The workshop simulates those characteristics of complex adaptive systems. Prediction and planning by the participants is virtually impossible. Responsiveness is necessary and trust is essential. Small changes are seen as important and are magnified through the non-linear feedback loops that exist during the workshop. This creates energy, understanding, responsiveness and a culture of care. The organization needs to be able to support those outcomes though its leadership and its systems. Then sustainability is assured and the subsequent growth in performance guaranteed.

The Dalrymple Bay Coal Terminal in north Queensland is a fine example of leadership understanding the business through the lens of complex adaptive systems theory and changing behaviour accordingly. The result of leadership based on this concept was an increase of 19 million tonnes per annum through the coal terminal over a four-year period – a staggering 73% increase. A further increase of 10 million tonnes per annum is being achieved through an additional ship loader. This capital investment is also adding greater complexity to the operation of the plant.

In summary, for the workshop to be successful the organization needs to support the business outcomes though its leadership and its systems. For sustainability to have any chance of success, and for subsequent growth in performance, leaders have to value responsiveness yet provide clear direction and boundaries. The direction and the boundaries themselves are shaped by agreed values.

Leaders need to desist from only seeing 'the workforce', 'the group', 'the team' and other big picture notions. What are needed are leaders who can pay attention to the individual and small changes in the organization while simultaneously observing the impact of small changes on the large system. Each person is unpredictable. On the other hand, each person has boundless energy and creativity. At the same time, individual actions have the potential to amplify and magnify as they travel through this non-linear system called the organization.

## Extraordinary Leadership Workshop - Stories

During the workshop, inspirational stories are read by either David, the staff person from the sponsor or a participant. Here are just a few that people seemed to find moving.

### The Magic Pebbles[62]

*One night a group of nomads were preparing to retire for the evening when suddenly they were surrounded by a great light. They knew they were in the presence of a celestial being. With great anticipation, they awaited a heavenly message of great importance that they knew must be especially for them.*

*Finally, the voice spoke, 'Gather as many pebbles as you can. Put them in your saddle bags. Travel a day's journey and tomorrow night will find you glad and will find you sad.'*

*After having departed, the nomads shared their disappointment and anger with each other. They had expected the revelation of a great universal truth that would enable them to create wealth, health and purpose for the world. But instead they were given a menial task that made no sense to them at all. However, the memory of the brilliance of their visitor caused each one to pick a few pebbles and deposit them in their saddle bags while voicing their displeasure.*

*They travelled a day's journey and that night while making camp, they reached in to their saddle bags and discovered every pebble they had gathered had become a diamond.*

*They were glad they had diamonds. They were sad they had not gathered more pebbles.*

---

[62] Author Unknown

## The Wheel and the Light[63a]

The master smiled and asked his disciples to imagine the wheel of a chariot. 'What determines the strength of a wheel in carrying a chariot forward?'

After a moment of reflection, his disciples responded, 'Is it not the sturdiness of the spokes, master?'
'But then why is it,' he rejoined, 'that two wheels made of identical spokes differ in strength?'

After a moment, the master continued, 'See beyond what is seen. Never forget that a wheel is made not only of spokes but also of the space between the spokes. Sturdy spokes poorly placed make a weak wheel. Whether their full potential is realised depends on the harmony between them. The essence of wheel making lies in the craftsman's ability to conceive and create the space that holds and balances the spokes within the wheel.'

## Maybe[63b]

A very old Chinese Taoist story describes a farmer in a poor country village. He was considered very well-to-do, because he owned a horse which he used for ploughing and for transportation. One day his horse ran away. All his neighbours exclaimed how terrible this was, but the farmer simply said 'Maybe.'

A few days later the horse returned and brought two wild horses with it. The neighbours all rejoiced at his good fortune, but the farmer just said 'Maybe.'

The next day the farmer's son tried to ride one of the wild horses; the horse threw him and broke his leg. The neighbours all offered their sympathy for his misfortune, but the farmer again said 'Maybe.'

The next week conscription officers came to the village to take young men for the army. They rejected the farmer's son because of his

---

63a,b Author Unknown

*broken leg. When the neighbours told him how lucky he was the farmer replied 'Maybe.'*

*The meaning that any event has depends upon the 'frame' in which we perceive it.*

## Sir Christopher Wren[64]

*The noted English architect Sir Christopher Wren once built a structure in London. His employers claimed that a certain span Wren planned was too wide, that he would need another row of columns for support. Sir Christopher, after some discussion, acquiesced. He added the row of columns, but he left a space between the unnecessary columns and the beams above.*

*The worthies of London could not see this space from the ground. To this day, the beam has not sagged. The columns still stand firm, supporting nothing but Wren's conviction.*

*Leadership is much more an art, a belief, a condition of the heart, than a set of things to do. The visible signs of artful leadership are expressed, ultimately, in its practice.*

Here are two stories related to the workshop.

## The 'Born Again' Participant

During one of the workshops a participant began the week displaying negative and destructive behaviours. He and a small number of his colleagues attacked the process in a passive, somewhat covert, yet aggressive way. This was far more harmful and effective in disturbing the workshop than overtly aggressive behaviour. This behaviour continued until half way into day 2 of the five-day workshop when it exploded as overtly aggressive behaviour. The person in question did not trust the organization that he was from and projected that view onto the workshop. He did not trust the organization so how could he trust the workshop to which the organization had given birth and actively sponsored? What was the organization up to? How was it going to take advantage of us? What sinister motives did it have?

---

[64] From *Leadership is an Art* by Max De Prees

Added to this, the local union official had suggested that the workshop was a plot by the company in question and gave enough information about the workshop, albeit out of context, to create fear among a small group of participants. The fact that this group responded to the stories created by that official suggested that the company had not allowed that participant to develop an identity with the company. Rather, he identified with the union concerned.

It was not until the fourth day that the participant discovered what the workshop was about. He discovered that it was about possibilities and not limits and constraints. It was about respect and dignity. It was about trusting and robust relationships. Finally, it was about choice – his choice to apply his discretionary energy or not. It was a truly emotional experience for a man that had a reputation as being tough and lacking in emotion. He was willing to share his emotion publicly. On the last day, the some senior managers from the company joined the group and that participant showed great courage and shared his journey of the week with the visitors. In fact, it was suggested by one of his colleagues that he should be appointed as sales director for the workshop. Such small changes are magnified throughout the system in a positive way. Not only did he become a committed employee after 25 years of battling the company but his new behaviour had a significant impact on others.

### Back at the workplace and The Rusty Conveyer Problem

A very important question is not only about what happens at the workshop, but what happens back in the workplace. This story is about the impact of the workshop on the workplace.

It was over two years since people from the organization were exposed to the workshop and we had the opportunity to observe a team of maintenance fitters in a large capital intensive plant having a regular team meeting. It was interesting to observe that they were sitting in a circle without the usual props that are found at meetings, such as tables, projectors, etc. They had embraced many of the processes learnt during the workshop and the conversations were intelligent with humour being used to support the conversation and not distract from it. Ideas, no matter how absurd they may have seemed at first were accepted and analysed. Those ideas were often built on to lead to superior solutions and to seize new opportunities to improve the business. In fact, all through the conversation people were constantly asking questions like 'Is it the best business solution?' or 'What will be the impact on the business?' Such questions were explored in an atmosphere of trust and an overwhelming commitment to the long-term success of the business.

At that meeting, the team was analysing a constant maintenance problem and looking for easier and cheaper ways to maintain the particular plant. The problem was that the piece of plant, a conveyor system, is located by the ocean and suffers from severe rusting. Traditionally, the organization spent somewhere in the order of a million dollars a year painting the conveyor system. The team set about looking for ways to effect savings in this area of maintenance and came up with the idea that the conveyor system could be manufactured in modules and when a module rusted out it could simply be replaced with minimum downtime for the operations and much less expenditure on painting. Not only did they generate this innovation, but the team set about to implement the idea rather than pass it up to a senior manager to take action.

It is through the workshops that the extraordinary leadership journey began for many people. It is a journey where the participants "regain the keys to their safes" and experience how productive it is to work in an environment of trust and complete open information. The workshops allowed people to let go of old paradigms and replace them with new ones that enabled individuals to make a difference in their organizations.

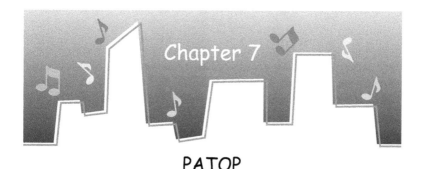

# PATOP

PHILOSOPHY, ASSUMPTIONS, THEORIES OF ORGANIZING AND PRACTICES

What is PATOP? It is a way for managers to test their 'walk' against their 'talk'. It is one of the most enjoyable experiences to go away on a management retreat and 'do' strategic planning. Due to excellent secretarial support and/or the use of technology on the retreat, it is not too difficult to write up and send around the policy documents with the requirements of the new strategies on them. However, when it comes to looking deeply at the structures, systems and processes that need to be changed, how often does this happen, and does it matter?

We hear from corporate colleagues that they are not always changed. We know from our various researches and workshops that yes, it seems to matter a lot to those faced with new rhetoric and old systems. We think that this is not as deliberate as people might think. Managers lead such pressured lives that they do not always 'think themselves' onto the shop or office floor. Even if they did, what could they use to check themselves out? PATOP is a framework for doing just that. People tell us that PATOP thinking is addictive and PATOP for individuals is well used for people to check their own personal vision against their jobs and other things in their lives.

You may want to know how PATOP came about. It was purely accidental. There was a not-very-nice report in the press. Workers up north had gone on strike, 'because their favourite ice cream flavour was not available'. The press made the most of this seemingly trivial event. Coincidentally, a few days later the same company was hailed in the press as an organization where 'workers are our greatest asset'. A lifetime of working with people and in witnessing many gestures such as strikes had taught us that often the gesture is a symptom or a signal of a deeper issue. How about if the ice cream was an example?

How about if, in a more general sense, there was little understanding of the things that would make a worker *feel genuinely valued*? And how would managers know this? How would they learn to interpret the signal? How would they know when an event was an example or even metaphor for a deeper message? The small hours of the morning must have some magic about them because somehow these thoughts came together then. I (Alma) designed a very practical tool which could be used to throw light on situations that develop.

**Why Philosophy?**

By far the most important aspect of the model was the surfacing of something that workers know intuitively. People in every walk of life philosophise. Philosophy is very important. When workers talk about the most important characteristics of managers (and vice versa) they can be relied upon to include somewhere near the top of their lists trustworthiness, integrity, honesty, and loyalty. What they are doing here is telling us what philosophers ask about. What makes a good life? (in our case at work). Workers have little choice but to accept management's philosophy. It is usually handed down in the vision statement. However, working life is practical and what workers look for is practical evidence of the vision in action.

The practical and the philosophical and the relationship between them - what should it be? Taking the talk as the philosophical and the walk as the practical, I reached back to the many years spent in the industrial north of England, listening and talking to labourers, tradesmen, factory workers, service workers (as well as teachers, shop workers, bank workers and others). One of the core issues, looking back, was disillusionment.

Managers (said people) did not do what the organization said they would do. So-called liberated organizations were very handy with straightjackets on autonomy, creativity, sociality and individuality. Managers (or foremen, supervisors etc.) often did not do what they preached they would do either. This was the message that came from the field. The metaphor of the battlefield was very much in evidence in those days. (The language was not too different either - tactics, strategy, frontiers of control, reporting lines, no doubt the reader can think of many more). Nowadays, we are more politically correct about some, but not all, of the language (see 'A phoenix or a feather duster'[65]) but has too much been done about the core issues? It seems a simple enough matter to take tacit or intuitive matters such as the core issues talked about amongst workers and transmit them to managers for translation into management development processes.

## The Thinking

Those readers who like a little history may be interested in how society and organizations came to be the way they are now. Society was modelled on physical things in nature (we are talking about over three hundred years ago). It was not necessary to interact with a tree to know it was a tree. This could be done objectively and impersonally. The problem was how to 'manage' people in society so that objective and impersonal methods could be replicated. The solution was for those in power at the time to develop structures and institutions (such as law, education, welfare, taxation). The next step was to get people to function in accordance with the requirements (rules, regulations, procedures) of the social institutions, of which organized work was one. A sociologist, solved this problem. It was clear to him that all civilized people would behave in a way laid down by those in power. They would be happy to obey 'norms' or expected behaviours of a well-integrated society. Those that were not could be labelled 'deviant' and dealt with accordingly.

Once agreement was made, then organizations could be thought of as machines. Each part had a role to play. Behaviour would be restricted to specified duties and the interest was in inputs and outputs. The process in between, where people made sense of the inputs and outputs was of no interest. It was called the 'black box', due to remain a mystery that no one really wanted to solve. Of course with the knowledge we have now, we know about quite a few things in the black box. We know there are feelings, values, needs, creative urges and, above all, wisdom and understanding. By safely containing these things in the box, it was possible to think about people as things and even as parts of the organizational machine.

---

[65] Whiteley, A. (1998) *A Phoenix or a Feather Duster*: Conference *'Realising Human Capital'*, Canberra, Australian Human Resource Institute .

Eventually, through industrialization the scientific dream was realized. An engineer, F.W. Taylor[66], developed his 'scientific management principles'. The story is too long to tell in detail but in essence he wrapped his designs around the notions of efficiency and measurement. He de-skilled jobs and placed people as extensions of machines such as conveyer belts and assembly lines. He devised efficient ways for people to move and he subtracted all social interaction (he hoped) from workplace design. He put in place hierarchies, supervision structures and performance measurements to reflect actual output. He developed sophisticated time and motion methods and was famous for his precise rules, procedures and instructions. He paved the way for many of the elements of mechanistic management we talked about in chapter three. Importantly, he established a language so that his theories could be preserved in words. Each time we talk about structures, systems and processes as though these can be seen concretely and objectively, even when those things are people, we 'speak his language'.

Clearly, life is not like that. People are not things. They have feelings, have moods, have fun and the occasional spat and generally are gloriously unpredictable. Because of the uniqueness of each situation we can say that life is momentary. It happens moment by moment and we all know that you can never get the moment back.

Realities are never concrete as they are always open to someone else's interpretation of them. True, those of us who have ever been surrounded by rules and regulations, manuals and instructions, policies and procedures may feel that they are as concrete as the Berlin wall. But look what happened to that. Behind most facts and figures in organizations lie relationships between the people who work on them. These relationships represent connections and interconnections between people. Connectivity is an area not often on the agenda of traditional training workshops. David's specialist work is unusual in that it is interested in helping people understand how they connect to themselves and others.

The PATOP model is built on the notion that what we see is not necessarily what we get, that the 'reality' we experience is perhaps a different reality from the one people suppose. The problem with

---

[66] Taylor, F. W. (1911) *Principles of Scientific Management* New York, Harper & Row.

those who think that they are designing a reality for others is that they also expect the reality to be enacted to suit. We think that this is one of the great myths of Taylorism; that managers, through structures, systems and processes, can prescribe a reality for others to follow. No doubt we have all suffered with that in the past, when we have felt that we are living out someone's private fantasy. That someone probably does not realise that what s/he gives out is not necessarily received, nor accepted as given, is not much comfort. We believe that there is a lens between a person's message or instruction, and that received by another. What might be some of the things within the lens? When we ask people they often say things like the amount of trust we have for the person (this seems to depend on the perception of his/her integrity and credibility). It will certainly be tempered by past experience with that person. These will have a strong role in translating the meaning of messages. This idea of managing meaning through the other person's lens is so important that it keeps coming up in many of the contexts we present. (See Figure 7.1)

The lens works both ways. What we perceive as reality is not necessarily valid for others. We have to work at it to see that ours and others' realities are as little distorted to the other as possible.

**What is said is**

**filtered**

**trust**

**values**

**personal history**

**experiences**

**culture**

**What is 'heard'**

Figure 7.1 What you say is not what I hear

Given that each reality is unique to the person holding it, the best we can do is to negotiate areas of meaning that we can agree on.

What we are describing here is the concept of a negotiated reality, not one that is prescribed. Through negotiation, some sense of shared understanding can be worked towards. The sense of matching, of alignment of meaning is a centrepiece of the PATOP model. It is designed to investigate whether the talk is matching the walk in terms of the symbols of meaning that structures, systems and processes have for others. We call these the walk. This is where the intention is translated into practice. It is where workers experience the talk in action. Workers, in enacting the authority structures, reward structures, communication systems and processes that make up daily life are trying them out for fit against declared intentions. Senior managers talk about the vision, the espoused values, of the organization. Workers are well placed to see whether the internal arrangements, what Fred Emery[67] would call the socio-technical systems, are designed to keep the faith with the values. PATOP is a way of expressing the match between talk and walk.

Just to summarise, PATOP was designed as a model for 'reflective thinking and diagnosis in organizations'[68]. It is a framework for matching *what is said* and *what is done* from either the viewpoint of the manager, worker or other involved groups such as customers. There is a strong focus on the alignment between an organization's Philosophy and Assumptions, (the theory of the organization) and its' Theories of Organizing and Practices (the practice of the organization). Hence the term PATOP. (Figure 7.2)

Why do we think that alignment is important? Listening to many organizational stories, at home and abroad, we soon find out that people need to be convinced that they are in line with the organizational 'cause'[69]. We hear of people going to war and dying for a cause so why should this be any different in working life?

---

[67] Emery, M., Ed. (1993) *Participative Design for Participative Democracy* Canberra, Centre for Continuing Education, Australian National University.
[68] Whiteley, A. (1999) *PATOP as a readiness for strategic decision making and change. An Occasional Paper for Advanced Theory in Business Seminar Series,* Perth, Western Australia, Graduate School of Business, Curtin University.
[69] Frost, P., Mitchell, V., Nord, W. (1992) *Organizational Reality: Reports from the Firing Line* Thousand Oaks, Sage.

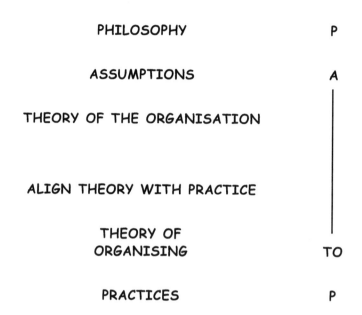

PHILOSOPHY                                    P

ASSUMPTIONS                                   A

THEORY OF THE ORGANISATION

ALIGN THEORY WITH PRACTICE

THEORY OF
ORGANISING                                    TO

PRACTICES                                     P

**Figure 7.2 Matching Theory and Practice**

In organizations, the cause takes the form of the philosophy of the organization. This is often found in vision statements, strategic themes or other key communications. From what we have heard in the last few years in our conversations with workers and managers, it seems clear that people expect the organization to be organized in such a way that the philosophy matches the structures, systems and processes that dictate how people relate to each other. Observing workers over a long period of time, one can not help but notice that the matching activity seems to be an integral part of their common-sense making. There seems to be an almost intuitive predilection for matching what is said with what is done. This happens both in terms of what managers 'say' both in words and writing and what they 'do' through the design of structures, systems and processes (Figure 7.3). The most transparent structure is the hierarchy which we refer to in detail (and passion) later in the book. Job levels, supervisory levels, and levels attached to things like decisions and problems tell their own story.

## The talk and the walk and where they live

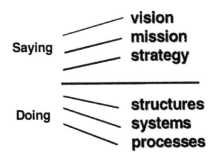

Figure 7.3 Saying and Doing

What about the organization that says it is an enabling learning organization? When you take a close look what do you find? Supervision is directive and prescriptive. Problem solving is of the 'taught solution' variety. The only decisions available to those at the bottom of the hierarchy are at the level of choosing the colour of toilet paper. And this is an enabling and learning organization? Well from where people are living, down in structural reality, the philosophy will soon be known for what it really is. The 'correct' philosophy, that is the one that matches reality, will replace the rhetoric of enablement. Workers will probably construe that the 'true' philosophy, the one in action resembles the rational economic vision of Taylor. (See Figure 7.4)

### Employees' Translation of the 'Real' Philosophy

There is more of a risk than may be realised in this translation process as cynicism sets in and eventually the very integrity is of those senior in the organization is questioned.

On the other hand, if what is said matches what is done on the shop floor then there will be a different story all together. Having passed the reality test, and assuming that the philosophy is acceptable, there are likely to be positive responses to decision implementation.

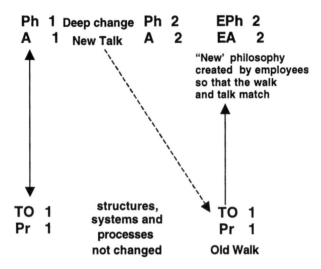

**Figure 7.4 Workers put things back in alignment**

This idea of thinking you are one thing, when clearly to the people receiving what you do you are finding something else entirely, brings us to another aspect of the PATOP model. This is the alignment or matching that goes on all the time between what managers say and what workers experience in the 'doing' part of things. The critical thinkers call this 'if-then' reasoning and because the theory is so interesting we have included a little of it here for your enjoyment.

There is always a dilemma in if-then thinking. The thing that comes before, taking the case of the Country and Western singer is 'if he is a Country and Western singer' logically leads to a consequence 'he wears spurs' (See Figure 7.5). The positive case can be taken as true. If he is not a Country and Western singer then he *may* wear spurs. On the other hand, he *may not* wear spurs. So in the negative case there is always a question. The answer is provided not necessarily by fact but by some sort of belief that has grown through experience. (See Figure 7.6)

For those who believe that everyone does or should love country and western singing then the above would be their 'truth'.

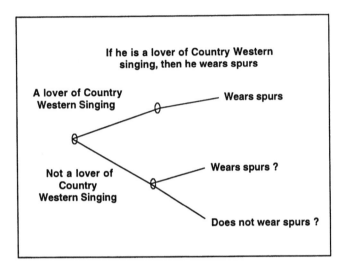

Figure 7.5 If-then thinking (1)

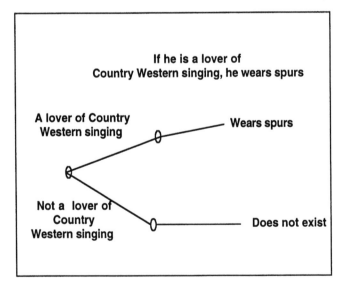

Figure 7.6 If-then thinking (2)

To take an example closer to working life. Let's take the case of the organization that says 'if its workers are a valued asset then 'they are given autonomy'.' If they really are valued then this will be evident in the structures, systems and processes wherein the evidence of autonomy lies. If they are not totally valued then in some cases we can see autonomy and in some cases we can not. (See Figure 7.7) This is no good to workers because only when autonomy is almost automatic will it be seen as sincere.

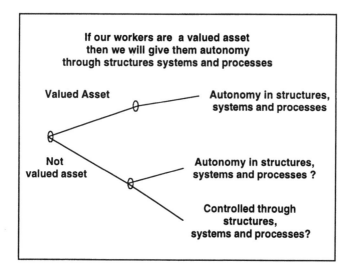

**Figure 7.7 Sometimes yes, Sometimes no = NO**

We are hypothesising now, but a way of looking at this is to think of the lens idea. Lets say that your observations lead you down the 'sometimes yes and sometimes no' route rather than the straightforward 'always yes' one. How would you judge what you were seeing?

Well, you might want to look at the initial premise, sometimes called the 'talk'. In this case it is the statement that workers are a valued asset.

What would be in the gap between what is said and what is received? (Figure 7.8)

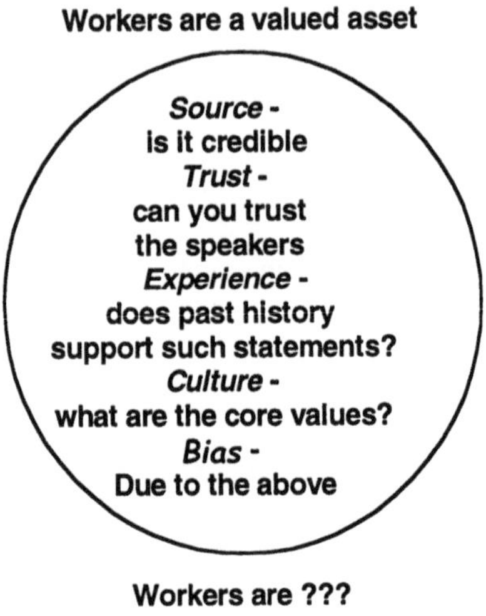

**Workers are a valued asset**

*Source -*
**is it credible**
*Trust -*
**can you trust
the speakers**
*Experience -*
**does past history
support such statements?**
*Culture -*
**what are the core values?**
*Bias -*
**Due to the above**

**Workers are ???**

**Figure 7.8 Judging what is said**

We have filled in such a gap with things that have emerged over the years from workers as important things upon which to base their judgement. Some of these are enabling, such as looking at the source and trust, but some are potentially disabling, such as the past experience. Why is this so? Well briefly, some research has suggested that people develop 'future memories'. What this means is that we gradually develop ways of looking at things and talking about them that are so strong that when we are faced with something new, it is not really new. We greet new events with our readymade views and these help give them meaning. An interesting idea that bears up strongly when we are having conversations with people is that we, as humans, have the unique ability to experience several 'virtual realities' at once[70].

We tested this out in a situation many of you will have experienced before or have that treat coming to you.

---

[70] Zohar, D. and I. Marshall (1994) *The Quantum Society: Mind Physics and a new social vision* London, Hammersmith.

We set the scene where a daughter had passed her driving test that day. She was seventeen and for the past year hundreds of dollars and a few family rows had gone into the effort. Now, on her seventeenth birthday, Dad, in a weak moment, had lent her his new car to go to a party on the strict understanding that she leave it there and get a taxi home. At one in the morning, just as Dad is going to bed the phone rings. It is his beloved daughter, hardly to be heard above the din, saying, 'Dad, the taxi won't come out here. I have promised three of my friends I'll take them home in the car. I haven't had much to drink so that should be OK with you?'

We asked the people helping us what was going through their minds. Lo and behold every one had several things going on at once. The sort of things? 'Oh God, I wish I had not lent her the car ... what if she has an accident ... just how much to drink has she had ... if anything happens to them I will never forgive myself ... I'm in trouble with her mother already ...' and so on.

Although this was more difficult for people to help us with, we asked them how much their past experiences had affected the way they looked at the situation. All said it did but they could not quite say how. That is not surprising as we take this for granted in our everyday life. It is important though, because when we think that we are giving someone a fair go we might actually be stacking the decks in favour of our biases and prejudged ideas. Our message to managers and workers alike is twofold. Firstly, there will always be a lens through which your message must pass, that is the person's personal way of seeing the world. Secondly, do not think that because a thing does not stand up as a fact that you can ignore it. Strong beliefs can represent reality and this reality is likely to be the one acted upon.

Within an acceptable match between philosophy and the theory of organizing, workers will see systems and processes, as well as the structures as legitimate ways to achieve agreed ends. Because this is where they live, in a world defined for them by norms, protocols, procedures and, above all institutionalised rules, workers have ultimate power in making them work – or otherwise. A reward system is one of the most tellingly symbolic of organizational systems. Monetary reward is symbolic. It says 'we are buying your time'. Money supported by conditions symbolises buying your time but giving you extra for which compliance is due. But what of the things that money can't buy? What do these symbolise? When we ask workers what it is that money can't buy *and* whether such things are important motivators, they typically say that the things money can't buy are very important.

They mention recognition that they (the workers) are respected human beings. They come up with some values like trust, integrity, autonomy, genuine feedback and being valued. In fact when doing the work for the 1995 book[71], the similarity of the importance and identity of shared values across just about every sort of industry you could think of was eerie. Given this information, it is an easy step to evaluating organizational philosophies such as scientific management and the effect they inevitably have on some of the most prized qualities in today's workforce, that is, individuality, creativity, and judgement.

**The First Question in PATOP**

The first question in PATOP is about the nature of the organizational philosophy. (See Figure 7.9) Is it plausible? By this we mean is it reasonable and acceptable in its consequences?

| | |
|---|---|
| **P** | **The human at work is rational/economic** |
| **A** | **Design for efficiency Reward with money** |
| **T** | **Scientific Management** |
| **O** | **Conveyers/assembly lines Extensions of machines** |
| **P** | **One person - one task Time and motion study** |

**Figure 7.9 Philosophy of The Human at Work**

---

[71] Whiteley, A. (1995) *Managing Change: A core values approach* Melbourne, Macmillan Education Australia Pty Ltd.

Let's take an example of a philosophy that, to us, is not only not plausible, but has been positively harmful for around one hundred years. Many will recognise this as the philosophy attached to Scientific Management principles.

**Rational Economic Philosophy**

Work, to be true to this philosophy, is a rational and economic undertaking and individuals are part of this mindset. It is efficient (and economical) to draw on the rational capability of humans at work. To be rational is to be in control. Marvin Wiesbord[72] in his book *Productive Workplaces: Organizing and Managing for Dignity, Meaning and Community* makes two contributions. He alerts us to the dangers of well meaning people whose beliefs are at odds with their designs and Taylor is his example. He shows us in stark clarity the results of a philosophy based on control. Frederick W. Taylor was one of the most influential, if not the most influential management theorist of his day. He developed a management philosophy based on scientific reasoning, in the doing of which he presented the human at work as a rational economic being. He began with himself, and rationality and self-control were an essential part of his life. He constantly tested himself for more efficient ways to live his life from the fastening of his (many) coat buttons to his inventions for adapting workers to efficient machines.

Weisbord (p26) has many sympathetic things to say about Taylor, '... a social reformer, who believed workers could produce more with less stress, achieve greater equity in their output and cooperate with managers for the good of society'. He also reports on Taylor's reputation (undeserved he thought) as 'a mechanistic engineer, dedicated to counting, rigid control, and the rationalisation of work, an unfeeling authoritarian who turned his own neurosis into repressive methods anathema to working people'. The PATOP model throws some light on the apparent contradiction within what Wiesbord calls 'the two Taylors'. Whatever Taylor's personal aspirations for workers, there is no evidence to show that he was not sincere in his thinking. It was the philosophy that dictated his

---

[72] Weisbord, M. R. (1987) *Productive Workplaces: Organizing and Managing for Dignity, Meaning and Community* San Francisco, Jossey Bass.

assumptions, although when we read the next quotation (Weisbord p30), the spirit of respect for workers does not shine through.

Young Taylor was appalled at the wasted effort exhausting work, long hours, petty dictators, arbitrary rules, inefficient methods and goofing off he found at Midvale Steel. He understood, having been one, why skilled workers rarely gave their best. Still, when he became a supervisor, he sought to dictate compliance, using the carrot and stick 'driving' methods of supervision.

The assumptions Taylor made about workers and productivity, underpinned his theory of management, sometimes called his management principles. This theory, in turn, informed his methods of organizing. As a serious inventor, he exercised his formidable design engineering skills on things like assembly lines, conveyer belts, shovels and other special tools. Workers had to adapt their bodies to these tools in order to get an efficient outcome. He also could not believe that workers could be good at more than one thing[73]. He talked about the supervisory equivalent of the 'first class manager'. Such a manager would have brains, education, technical knowledge, physical strength, energy, grit, honesty and so on. He could not envisage that one manager could have all of these traits so he chopped the job into eight discrete tasks, one for each characteristic of the first class person. A gang boss set up jobs, a speed boss picked the best tools, a quality control inspector set standards, a repair boss maintained equipment, a route clerk wrote out production lists and so on until we come to the discipline boss who handled 'insubordination or impudence'. The one thing that these managers had in common was that they were using their brains: 'managers think'. This 'deskilling of character' was to manifest itself into Taylor's deskilling of jobs also. Workers had a different quality: 'workers do'. 'Managers think and workers do' was (and still is) a well-recognised syndrome on the shop floor. Because efficient 'doing' was best attained under strictly controlled and repetitive conditions, then one person to one task was added into the equation. We will say more about this when we talk about Fred Emery's design principles. Let's explore Taylor's rational economic ideas using PATOP.

---

[73] Taylor, F. W. (1911) *The Principles of Scientific Management* New York, Harper & Row.

**Applying PATOP to Rational Economic Philosophy**

Philosophy: the human is a rational economic being and as such will be in harmony with scientific management principles of prediction, control and objectivity. The human is a part of a wider society which is, in turn, scientific, objective and concrete[74].

Assumption: rational economic people were best rewarded by individual incentives (money). To make as much of it as possible, all extraneous, messy and non-productive movements needed to be eliminated. This of course mainly refers to the social side of life. Chatting, developing camaraderie, installing some human elements in the work was not predictable or controllable, therefore not efficient.

Theory, design for efficiency and control: 'managers must gather in all of the great masses of traditional knowledge which in the past has been in the heads of the workmen and in the physical skill and knack of the work-men [and reduce it to] rules laws and formulae'[75]. As many writers have pointed out Taylor was not interested in worker participation. He stood for rational control, and for this read managerial control, of workers through division of labour, deskilled tasks and machine-led movements.

Organizing, the concept of the human as an extension of a machine, was borne out by Taylor's inventions to go along with his theory. Conveyer belts, assembly lines, specially shaped shovels (that required controlled ways of moving) were practical outcomes of his theorising about effective management. Taylor helped pioneer time and motion study, a management control system that sought to bend human action to the will of efficient work practices[76].

Practices, separation of thinking and doing: in practice this meant sepa-ration of the planning and coordinating functions from the physical ones. Work roles became differentiated. Tasks were done in a rigid order. Individuals had specialised skills. Responsibility was for one's own task. There were well preserved differences in status (managers supervise workers' actions). Supervision was both internal (inspection) and external.

---

[74] Whiteley, A. (1995) *Managing Change: A core values approach* Melbourne, MacMillan Education Australia Pty Ltd.
[75] Copley 1923 in Weisbord 1987, p64).
[76] Gilbreth, F. B. (1911) *Motion Study* New York, Van Nostrand.

The one thing we can say about this brief excursion into Taylorism (apart from the fact that he was a brilliant engineer and inventor, a pioneer in management thinking and a person sincerely dedicated to worker-management cooperation – of a sort) is that his philosophy was absolutely in alignment with his assumptions, theories of organizing and practices. Yet many people on the shop floor would agree that his thinking left the bulk of worker intelligence untapped and the practical ability of managers unwanted, clearly a waste of human capability. As Taylor believed that workers could not design tools, work out and plan tasks, much less develop systems methods policies and procedures, it was not surprising that the only way to ascertain results was to have the 'first class minds' of foremen and managers in control.

Having applied the PATOP model you can see that Taylor was actually in alignment. His talk matched his walk. So what was wrong? Just the small matter of getting it wrong about the nature of the human at work. Yes, we are rational and yes we are economic beings. However, the rational economic is by no means deterministic. Any of you that have metaphorically cut your career throat on a principle (like us) must admit that the rational can easily give way to the emotional just as economic rewards can give way to the pat on the back from someone we respect. We are whole people. We care about more than ourselves. We are social as well as self-centred. In fact social needs are a very human thing. The human at work as a social being would be nearer the mark sometimes than the human as rational economic.

This was the basis of philosophy presented by one of the greatest management thinkers (and an Australian), Fred Emery. Emery was part of a movement called Human Relations, often referred to as 'Tavistock' after the institute in which a very different philosophy was promoted. First, pioneers like Kurt Lewin found that when people participated in deciding issues these were likely to work. He and various management thinkers of the day discovered the existence of 'the social group' and the sort of solidarity and power that could develop from group relationships. Through various researches and experiments it became fairly clear that it was foolish to introduce any technical system without due care and attention being given to the social preferences of those who would have to use it.

Back to Fred Emery[77] and an alternative PATOP. Fred and his colleagues coined a term, socio-technical systems. From the beginning the worker was recognised as a very different being than that in Taylor's thinking. Here the nature of the worker was as a person having skill and brainpower and the desire to cooperate as part of the social life of work.

**P**   The human at work is
        A valued asset

**A**   Money and feedback

**T**   Participative
        Management

**O**   Core structures
        Informal and formal
        Systems/processes

**P**   Many skills in use
        Machines follow people

**Figure 7.10 Philosophy of the Human at Work**

Let's take a very different version of the human at work. Let's think of him or her as 'The human at work is a valued asset' (Figure 7.10).

**Socio-technical Systems Theory**

The work of Fred Emery[78] and his colleagues is well described in the book *Participative Design for Participative Democracy*. This one idea led to an overturning of Taylorist principles and a new theory called socio-technical systems. Emery, like Taylor, referred to 'first principles' of management and he used Taylorist principles in counterpoint to his Design Principle 2 theory.

In Design Principle 1, as we see in Figure 7.11 all of the elements of scientific management are present. How easy it is to substitute a person who is simply attached to a task.

---

[77] Emery, F. E. and Trist, E.L. (1973) *Towards a Social Ecology* London, Tavistock.
[78] Emery, M. Ed. (1993) *Participative Design for Participative Democracy* Canberra Centre for Continuing Education, Australian National University.

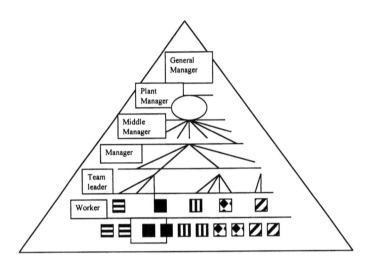

**Figure 7.11 The worker as a redundant part**

But that is not the biggest insight from Design Principle 1. It is much more costly than it seems. We talked earlier about the disturbance that comes with uncertainty and far from agreement. Let us take the example where someone does not turn up for work. You can count out the other workers who are alongside as they are attached to a task or a function. Therefore the problem has to be solved from above, thereby taking control up one level. Not only that, but there really is only one way to solve it. This is to make sure that there are 'spare' (also redundant) parts always to hand in the system. Let us use the example David gives of BHP Steel in the Shackled by Bureaucracy chapter (Ch. 9). The organization had many spare 'human parts' and some people were there to do the 'just in case' jobs. Then the organization during the 1980's decided to 'lose some weight' (and relieve itself of its redundant parts). So, we ask, how would the supervisor solve the problem without 'spare parts' to hand. The answer was, not to enrich jobs and expand horizons but to engage external contracting companies to fill the slot.

Now let us look at Design Principle 2, Figure 7.12.

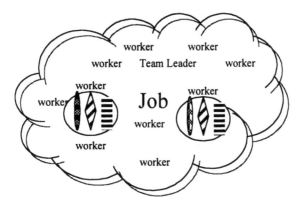

**Figure 7.12 Each Worker has Many Functions**

In Design Principle 2, one person would have many skills to bring to a job. Not all of them would be needed simultaneously. Some of them would be required to function 'on the day'. Others would be held in reserve to be produced when needed. By limiting the requirements to one function per person, (as in Design Principle 1), any others went to waste. As well as functions, Weisbord[79] tells us, Taylor squeezed out qualities such as human variability, personal self control, worker creativity and above all worker discretion. Learning from a coal mining study, (another story) Emery and his colleague, Eric Trist, found that miners were good at making frequent independent decisions that were often outside of the formal job description.

Given the scope and permission to create, the miners in their study soon made technical breakthroughs. These were enormous. They resembled the idea of a traditional army group versus a tactical response one. In the tactical response group, people are treated as scarce and valued resources. It is assumed that many functions and skills are present. This is so that versatility and flexibility can be utilised to meet rapidly changing circumstances. In the mining study, the miners had a secret weapon: themselves as a social group. They showed that people who pull together and care about each other can perform better. Cooperation for both

---

[79] Weisbord, M. R. (1987) *Productive Workplaces: Organizing and Managing for Dignity, Meaning and Community* San Francisco, Jossey Bass.

personal and mutual benefit goes with the social responsibility to be a good group member.

We come to a major assumption of socio-technical systems theory. People are rewarded by designs that let the social interact with the technical. Rational is replaced by social. Economic is replaced by mutual benefit. Under the socio-technical system assumption, the human was considered as more than either a brain (in the case of management) or arms and legs (in the case of workers). The idea of social values came into play. People valued learning as much as possible about the whole job. They valued social cooperation. They had a taste of being allowed to self control and they valued that too. Fred Emery looked outside the immediate and sterile world of control systems and introduced the appealing idea of open systems. Basically this means that everything affects everything else. Nothing is ruled out. One-way communication does not exist. One-way responsibility cannot exist. People, technical tasks, outside influences are all part of a whole. What affects a part affects the whole.

In place of the line of cause and effect comes the spiral of information. The centrepiece in open systems thinking is feedback. All feedback is information. Circular feedback, positive feedback and even negative are all useful. Feedback sparks thinking. Hopefully, it might just result in something creative or innovative. Moreover, the idea of one best way is not possible in the open system. There are many ways and most of them can work especially if they are owned by those involved.

So how would socio-technical systems theory look in a PATOP analysis?

### Applying PATOP to Socio-technical Systems Theory

Philosophy: the human at work is a social being. S/he is a scarce resource, a learner, co-operator and a co-organizer.

Assumptions: as social learners people are best rewarded by the relational job incentives. People are trusted to offer their full range of knowledge and skills to best organize the job. Chatting, developing camaraderie, installing some human elements in the work is encouraged. There is trust in individuals and groups to make interactions work for them to increase productivity.

Theory — Design Principle 2: The theory is one of participation and democracy. There are diverse ways to do the job. The job is designed in accordance with Design Principle 2, socio-technical theory. The only redundancy in this theory is in the skills not currently being used at any one time. Each person has multiple skills and these are on offer when needed, some of them being temporarily redundant at any one time. The theory of this design is that the more you have in the way of autonomy, participation in decisions and responsibilities, the more you can respond to anything that comes along without being held up and sending for a 'specialist'.

Practices: Workers are grouped around a job. Each person has multiple skills. The skills can be drawn on as decided by the group. Internal leadership provides the bulk of supervision. Worker roles are interchangeable to as large a degree as practicable. The task order is flexible. There is an equal status within the group. Shifts integrate to allow the social and the technical to overlap.

### Using PATOP to Test Assumptions

Two more quick PATOPs show how the assumptions held by managers can result in very different ways of managing. They are based on Douglas McGregor's[80] Theory 'X' and Theory 'Y' (see Table 7.1). A manager is a person who has certain assumptions about the worker. These assumptions cause the manager to design structures, systems and processes accordingly. Because they are designed in accordance with the assumptions, the results are self fulfilling prophecies.

The fascinating thing about theory X and theory Y is that when managers are asked which they are, they always say (the talk) theory Y. When you look at the actual ways in which they organize (the walk), especially in terms of giving responsibility and making decisions, not to mention solving problems, it is hard to see many theory Y managers around. Why is this? Well it is easy to think of theory X managers as monsters but there is the kind of person we have all met who is the kindly sort. This person has been on the shop floor for twenty years or more, has seen many people come a cropper

[80] McGregor, D. (1966) *Leadership and Motivation: essays of Douglas McGregor* Cambridge, Mass, M.I.T. Press.

and feels s/he is doing a really good turn by protecting the rest of us. Such a person's intentions are good but lurking in there is a little of the theory X theorising that we just are not that smart, have not been around too long and need a bit of gentle control and direction. In other words, without knowing it is possible to be a theory X in theory Y clothing.

| Theory X | Theory Y |
|---|---|
| Philosophy: Workers inherently dislike work and where possible will attempt to avoid it. | Philosophy: workers view work as a natural thing and get enjoyment from it. |
| Assumptions: need to be coerced, controlled, or threatened with punishment to achieve goals. Reward is money and security. | Assumptions: can allow self direction but need to gain commitment. Workers will take responsibility, are creative and can make decisions. |
| Theory: theory of control | Theory: theory of cooperation |
| Organizing: formal direction in the form of orders, instructions. Clearly defined tasks with little discretion. Organize for compliance. Organize for tasks | Organizing: some direction gradually leading to autonomy. Allow some discretion in tasks, both when and how to do them. Organize for cooperation. Organize for jobs. |
| Practice: work to rule, follow instructions, wait for supervisor to direct, 'put in the time'. Led from above. | Practice: flexibility allowed in working schedules. Decisions are made both by workers and managers. Supervisors often consulted rather than directing. Led from above and within. |

Table 7.1 Theory X and Y

Over the years, we have noticed that in spite of incoming information to suggest otherwise, managers and workers continue to engage in the same rounds of dialogue. These, we think are usually about some aspect of the 'walk' area. That is arguments or discussions about concrete things, rosters, job schedules or content, communication problems processes for reporting on performance and so on. We call this the edifice or the building of the organization (see Figure 7.13). What we have not seen too much of in the past, especially within the remit of workers is questioning or discussion at the foundational level. So, continuing with the building analogy, as long as serious cracks do not show in the building, the foundation is assumed to be good. By foundation of course we mean philosophy. Another way of saying this is that we see many (and often in the past, bitter), questions asked about the more superficial things but virtually none about the deep things such as 'who are we, what do we believe in and value'?

This results in very important strategies like downsizing, upsizing, (capsizing? only joking) outsourcing and the many more restructuring inventions being considered in operational terms. What do we downsize? To whom do we outsource? How do we relate to contractors? And other such what and how questions.

Foundational questions, you could think of them as systemic ones, would be something like these. How would cutting off limbs affect the character of the organization? What will our new configuration do to the community of workers and customers who interact with us? Who are we now that we are dismantled? And the questions everybody asks and apparently few people answer - *why are we doing things this way?*

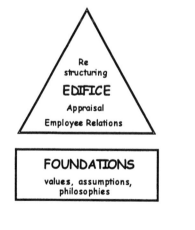

Questions about management practices are asked around the theory of organising tea breaks, rostering, holidays, appraisal scores, manning, job designs, promotions

In doing the above, the old foundations are validated, critical questions are deflected and critical self-appraisal is avoided

Figure 7.13 Where are the important questions asked?

The 'edifice' thinking does not apply only to organizations in the general sense. It applies to all of us in our team relations, the way we think about the 'whys' of our actions and the way we continually elevate things to the 'what' and 'how' conversations. After you read this, you can check it out in your organization. Does it encourage deep questioning? A little later, we will talk about sceptical thinking and if this occurs at the deepest level of an organization, then that organization is probably a 'learning organization' in more than words. Conversely, it becomes self evident that an avoidance of deep level thinking causes rigidity and inflexibility with little real opportunities for learning.

### Using PATOP to Manage Change

These issues become important in the face of change. We are going to assume, for the sake of the next PATOP idea that the organization is operating at the philosophical level and that it can and does challenge its own assumptions. Change automatically alters the alignment of PA and TOP. It must do because of the time it takes to translate the changed philosophy and assumptions into new theories of organizing and correspondingly changed practices.

The insights that brought about this extension of the PATOP model came from the observation that with strategic planning usually came directives for change from senior management. Given the need to keep the organization in alignment, it would have been reasonable to assume that an accompanying change in structures, systems and processes would have been presented, at least in outline. We have observed that this was the exception rather than the rule. There seemed to be, in many cases, very little in the way of planning to manage the drift brought about by changing the philosophy and assumptions upon which the organization had been previously operating. The one thing we know for sure is that there *will* be drift as the new philosophy moves away from the old structures systems and processes. What needs to be worked out is what an acceptable time for drift would be, given the organization's history of and ability to manage change, to secure commitment to decisions and to communicate with those responsible for implementation. (See Figure 7.14)

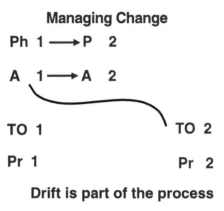

**Managing Change**

Ph 1 ⟶ P 2

A 1 ⟶ A 2

TO 1                    TO 2

Pr 1                    Pr 2

**Drift is part of the process**

**Figure 7.14 Managing drift**

There is an interesting dilemma for organizations here. Intuitively there is a sense of completion in the formulation stages of strategic change. This comes out of the sort of linear thinking that divides formulation activities and implementation ones. Consummation of plans can only happen upon implementation. Implementation happens on the shop floor and it does not happen naturally. It has to be managed. This calls for analysis of the organization's history, employees' attitudes towards change and the extent of the change in terms of how it might affect current working conditions. Thinking of drift as a continuum, if an organization has a history of stability, conservativism and an attitude to change that sees it as a not-so-necessary evil then it will be at one end of the continuum. This is the end that has the farthest to go to match the new PA to a correspondingly new TOP. If the organization is dynamic and its attitude to change is that it is part of daily life then it will be at the other end of the continuum, with a short drift period. Two main activities are involved in the change process. These are modifying the existing structures, systems and processes and communicating the change arrangements to the workforce.

The final PATOP extension has proved to be very useful in everyday life in organizations. We have called it 'multiple perspectives' and it has an intuitive appeal. We were involved in a research on the waterfront at Fremantle[81] at the time when there was a national controversy and outcry involving very different groups. Farmers, managers, unions, community groups and government were all involved. There were as many PATOP's as there were groups. Taking four of them, unions, managers, government and community groups we look at several perspectives. (See Figure 7.15)

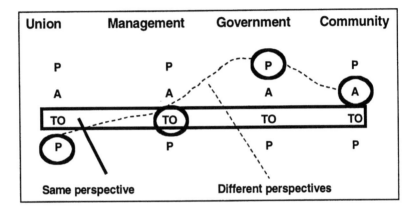

————————— Is the desirable conversation, that is all conversing at the same level.

------------- Is the abortive conversation that takes place when each participant is talking at a different level.

**Figure 7.15 Multiple Perspectives: Different conversations**

In particular, we looked at conversations both when these groups were together and when they were 'conversing' in the media. As you can see in Figure 7.15, each group was pursuing its area of interest. Therefore, there were four monologues happening.

It is like 1+1+1+1 = 1. Users (or should we say addicts) of PATOP tell us that the ability to very quickly a) diagnose that different conversations are happening and b) find ways to bring people together

---

[81] Whiteley, A. M. and McCabe M. (2001) *Sustainable Change: A Case on the Waterfront,* Perth, Australia, Vineyard Publishing.

is very useful to them. They say that these simple abilities have helped their negotiation skills.

This then is the PATOP model. Just before I leave this (it is Alma speaking) I will tell you a funny story. At the time of the telling, there was only the first part of the model, the alignment part. I launched it with some trepidation to some managers in my class. It went well and I was feeling full of myself and oh so clever. That is until about halfway home on the freeway I started thinking of home and of my family life. Did I walk the talk? Well I was always saying at home how my family life came first, how I go to work to help the family etc. etc. etc. That was my talk sorted out. I then looked at my walk, especially things like going home for dinner, being home in the evening for company, or even the odd time at weekends.

As I rarely made it home before eight thirty or nine and that sometimes included weekends, I could hardly say that my walk lived up to my talk. So I got home and said, 'I'm going to change. I've realised that I don't live up to my rhetoric.' My partner said, 'What's wrong ... what's going on ... why are you suddenly feeling guilty after all this time?' It took a lot convincing that all that had happened was a revelation due to PATOP. Anyway, the moral of the story is that the model can work in the personal life. From the next day, I changed my work habits. I came home for dinner, brought the laptop computer back and although I still work in the evenings, I can contribute to family life.

There have been a substantial number of reports in from people who have used PATOP for family and work relationships and in planning what they should do with their lives.

**PATOP for the workgroup**

So far, we have talked about PATOP more as a management tool than a worker tool, although workers are performing their own 'matching' analysis of the organizational talk and walk.

It is a very handy tool also for such activities as team work. In a way, developing a team is very like developing an organization. Many teams, however, do not design themselves at all. They have or are given a task and they go hell for leather to complete the task. Yet we know from as early as the 1930's and the 'Hawthorn Experiments'[82] that what we call process is a key component in team success. Process is basically the way people go about things. The best possible process is like a chain with no weak links. Each separate component is taking the strain of the load but it takes the whole chain to pull effectively. You've all heard the saying 'a chain is only as strong as its weakest link'. What does it take to make everyone pull together, knowing that within the team, talents are likely to be unevenly distributed, people will have off days, information and instructions about the task will not always be clear and forthcoming? Well of course the short answer is work - of a special sort, that is team design work. Here is how such a team might go about its work.

**Vision:** To be a high performing team where we care for each other

**Basic rules:** Set high standards, see to the logistics, be creative, look out for each other.

**Team structures:** Two level hierarchy. The expert on the current aspect of the task takes the leadership role.

Team subcommittees to solve problems and make proposals to bring to the team for approval. Decisions will be made on a 'convincing argument' basis and there may not always be consensus. However, everyone has a voice and nothing is ruled out before discussion.

Committee membership rotates according to the problem or decision at hand. A spokesperson will be nominated based on his/her 'talk' skills to interact with management, customers or others as needed.

**Team systems:** The team information system will be coordinated by the current team leader and the sub-committees. Daily scanning will be the responsibility of whoever is not essential to the task that day. The team will seek training on the use of internet or other information methods.

This team places logistics high on its agenda. Training in this will be given to all existing team members as well as new members.

---

[82] Mayo, E. (1930) *A New Approach to Industrial Relations* Boston, Division of Research, Graduate School of Business Administration, Harvard University.

The team communication system will be largely informal. There are three central skills that the team will concentrate on. These are: active listening, sceptical thinking and supportive communication. Training will be needed in these areas. Particular attention will be given to creative problem solving and each team member is encouraged to produce new ideas or ways of looking at the task.

The team performance management system will include the setting of goals and targets. This will be done in conjunction with management (that is if management is not already part of the team). The team will take responsibility for coaching and counselling and will ask for expert help, making a clearly presented case for the extra resource. Monitoring will be ongoing and will be in relation to the rhythm of the task.

**Team processes:** The major process aspect will be the building and maintaining of relationships within the team. As the team will be diverse in both personalities and learning styles, training will be needed in making team members self aware. The model below will be adopted by the team (Figure 7.16).

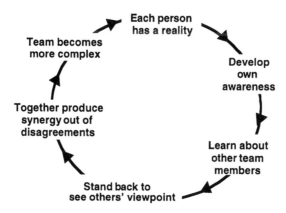

Figure 7.16 Team Diversity model

This model looks deceptively easy. The words 'working with diversity' sound easy too. Yet this is one of the most difficult areas for team-work. The reason to follow the model is no problem. It does not take genius to know that people have to give a bit and adapt to each other. What, in our view, is grossly underestimated is the strain involved in incorporating different ideas or points of view into one's own personality at more than a superficial level. What this is asking of us is that we stop being the straightforward, single-minded person that we have been up to date, throwing off ideas and opinions that do not fit our point of view. Instead, we become creatures of contradiction. Imagine a manager, embracing (not necessarily agreeing with but embracing all the same) a union viewpoint, a production engineer taking on board a marketing manager's perspective or workers incorporating the concerns of payroll clerks into their own realities.

In a broad brush sense, we think that this would be very difficult to achieve. The reason is that it goes against the 'one best way' thinking that most of us have been fed since infancy. However, step-by-step it becomes easier. For example, how does one become self aware? This takes courage in itself. I am not too sure that I was absolutely ready to find out that I was an introvert, especially considering that the bulk of my work is socially interactive. I had always considered myself as a practical person and found out that I am a theorist/reflector instead. On the team roles front I have always known that I am a bit of a challenger but was pleased to find that I am a finisher too. Absolutely the best thing about becoming self aware through the use of various techniques was that I was forced to think very carefully about the areas I needed to avoid if I could.

I have learned, not to perfection, how to incorporate 'other selves' in to my own thinking. I learned to recognise activists/pragmatists (opposite to theorist reflector) very quickly through their conversational style. I have learned to ask 'when, where, how, who, what is the plan'? Really, I would prefer a comprehensive briefing on background and ideas. I have developed some skill in taking a back seat and providing a supportive role as well as keeping my challenger skills for when needed. These things do not sound much but they are difficult to achieve and they take time. The strength of this ability to become more complex team members is incalculable. A team would be quite justified in considering this ability to be a competitive edge.

Help would need to be sought for things to develop self-awareness such as personality types, learning styles, team roles and 'embracing differences' skills.

Still on team processes, the team will need to develop some protocols, that is, team norms. These will be worked out by the team but will be open to review and modification when any team member thinks that it is time. These norms should reflect our basic rule of 'looking out for each other'.

The above is just an idea of how a team might go about designing itself. PATOP can then be employed every week or so to check out whether the design is being lived up to. This calls for a ruthlessness not currently found in too many organizations. We have noticed a sort of gentle collusion or co-dependency between managers and workers but also between team members. No one really wants to rock the boat and the major goal is one of keeping each other happy rather than being each other's sternest critic. However, the key to any effective team is an enthusiasm for what we might call 'deconstructive' thinking. The desire to pull something to bits that is working adequately goes against the grain of the 'if it isn't broken, don't fix it' slogan. However, we believe that the very best product, idea or system is only best at that moment. The high performing team knows that 'we've achieved the best – now lets look at the next mountain to climb'.

A fun thing to do immediately is to stop reading this book and do your own individual PATOP. What is your personal philosophy about life? What are the things you value? Work on down and have a look at the things going on in your life and see whether you are out of alignment with yourself. We think that it is much better to change things like activities and even jobs than to bend your philosophy to match them.

# Notes

## LEARNING THROUGH REFLECTION

The theory, workshop and stories, supply (we hope) ample material for refection. To make things easier, we have written a short summary of the central concepts taking us from mechanistic to transformational and on to complex approaches to leadership. Using this summary will help you decide many things not only about implications for your organization but also for yourself. What are the expectations people have of you and do they help you, as a leader, meet the constant challenges of a complex world?

### The New Leader

Times have changed. We are experiencing more pressures and problems and find that old ways of managing no longer work. We hope that by introducing you to our favourite scholars, and adding our own experiences, has broadened organizational possibilities for you.

We believe that strategy, change and leadership go hand in hand, and use complexity theory to help guide us in this changing world we live in. We recognise that adapting to constant change, needs a new leadership style – one that we call *Extraordinary Leadership*. This style of leadership doesn't use Newtonian control from outside or above to manipulate, it works 'within' the organization, managing feedback loops and ensuring that they are rapid, comprehensive, and short cycled. Information and experiences are shared to create a continuing transformational system. *Extraordinary Leaders* know how to transform variables to create new opportunities, possibility, innovation etc. One could say they choose to take advantage of every unpredictable variable (external tension and uncertain variables such as people within the organizational system) rather than control them. If the organization ignores these variables however, there is of course risk involved, because amplifying effects can manifest negatively or positively. We argue, what greater risk is there than ignorance? Ignorance of the scientific evidence which supports that human systems are complex adaptive systems with rules that change? Ignorance of intangible assets? Ignorance of possibility? This is high risk.

Although we recognise that Mechanistic (Newtonian) Management gives us the license to operate and is intended to limit and control, we hope that we have demonstrated that it does not provide the leadership for organizations that exist in an environment which is far from certainty and agreement. At best, it provides management.

We have uncovered the pitfalls of mechanistic mindset in relation to infinite variability, by addressing the following traditional strategies: rules, regulations and procedures; defined rigid structures; rational problem solving processes and control; detailed plans and budgets; performance management from above; and bureaucratic structure.

The transformation edge, which lies far from certainty and agreement, can be viewed positively in light of complexity theory. It is the tension at this edge that drives us to new frontiers, and creative and innovative thinking. But how do we lead an organization to new possibilities from a management style which promotes limitation? Simply put, we can't.

Through observing behaviour of 'strange attractors' we can to some degree understand the natural pull that occurs when initial conditions are set in place, at the same time allowing amplifying effects to occur. Converting this to organizational language, we embrace the paradox of the certain/normal and the uncertain/extraordinary. We also understand that old paradigms need to be shattered for new ones to emerge, and we propose an approach based on values, which affects the whole of the organization regardless of whether the positioning is certain or uncertain.

From this values base, we have developed from our extensive research and experience, a guide to *Extraordinary Leadership* - a practical method for leaders. This is based on the premise that organizations want performance (not limitation) and that performance = direction + willingness. Without willingness, people will not deliver discretionary energy. So let's briefly take you on a medley of dances to review our journey.

**Relationships** - one needs to first respect intangibles in order to appreciate the value of relationship. We have much evidence to support that intangible assets make the difference between an outstanding organization and one that isn't. We cannot emphasise enough the importance of this. We need to go on a journey of discovery ourselves first, and then build relationships with others to effectively respond to the changing environment. A part of this development is the recognition and acceptance of tension and paradox, along with the recognition of variability not only of the people who form the organizations we are in, but also of the variability we face with customers, and the uncertainty in the world. We have seen how people self-organize in crisis situations, such as September 11. These show how tension can indeed be a positive thing, in that it forces people to stretch themselves.

Sharing information is fundamental to the non-linear feedback loops important to any system in the quest of sustainability. In order to gain valuable information, we rely on robust relationships, and in doing so need to value feeling equally with thinking. Communication is essential to information exchange and we hope that Argyris'[83] 'espoused theory and theory in practice' adds to your understanding in this area and provides useful knowledge for development. Also, we hope that a connection has been made between emotional competencies and business success. Listening, feedback and acknowledgement, along with behaving in line with espoused values is so important. We see through attachment theory that people are different and variable in their relating style as well as personality, and so we need to adapt not only to the unpredictable world around us but also to those different from us.

We encourage communities of practice and networks, to share knowledge, drive strategies, generate new opportunities, solve problems, promote best practice, develop competencies, recruit and retain talent. We also encourage 'partnerships' featuring interdependency, rather than placing responsibility in the level above. We look at various forms of structure, and the deception of restructure. We see in many organizations, loosely coupled systems held together by organization culture and a sense of identity. We recognise and value the *informal system* in this sense.

---

[83] Argyris, C. (1989) *Reasoning, Learning and Action* San Francisco: Jossey-Bass

As we move onto *Extraordinary Leadership* strategies, understanding that underlying all of these is the development of robust relationships, we make a case for each of the following: information; identity and purpose; vision and values; trust and support; double loop learning not blame; customer focus; personal responsibility; boundaries and guidelines; flexible budgets to guide; and performance management from a broad base.

We will briefly review our conclusions of these.

### Ten Conclusions

**Information** - crucial to organizations performing in an extraordinary way. It is the life blood of organizations, and needs to be readily accessible at all levels. The main functions of managers are facilitation, leadership and management of information (gathering, analyzing and feeding back).

**Identity and purpose** – alignment between the individual and the organization. Leaders need to provide challenging employment to gain passionate commitment. This leads to discretionary energy reflected in bottom line performance. In areas of uncertainty it is important to minimise external rules and allow control to come from within to enable flexible responses. Self-control through commitment is better than seeking compliance.

**Vision and Values** – the act of creating a desirable future and how we would like to be with each other. Values are shared norms and beliefs that govern how we interact. Tension arises when people behave differently to the values and these are a major cause of mistrust. Managing by values from within rather than external rules is far more effective and provides the self-control to meet infinite number of unpredicted situations. Managing by values also includes consequences for those who display values contrary to agreed values. As stated earlier in the book, Meg Wheatley claims that if information is the centre stage, then vision is the field around it - a field that permeates the organization, rather than a destination. Executive managers need to share their vision without enforcing it on their employees. It is necessary for teams to create their own vision and values and structures and processes need to be in line with them.

**Trust and Support** - people need to feel valued. Since the mechanistic model sees people as machines, we can expect poor results. We must acknowledge that when we employ people we get a pair of hands plus a mind that includes the emotional part – commonly known as the heart. Mutual trust is the essence of a high performing organization. Robust relationships lead to open & honest communication that leads to trust over time. If there is no trust, then only 'safe' information will be shared. This leads to poor problem solving and decision-making, then sub-optimal performance and a blame culture develops.

**Double Loop Learning and Not Blame** - blame culture is very destructive to organizations – people withhold information that causes cover-ups. It also kills trust, improvement and creativity and eventually damages relationships. Blame culture leads to victim behaviour where people demonstrate a lack of personal responsibility.

Learning from mistakes encourages people to experiment and innovate. Double loop learning goes beyond solving the symptoms and problems; it changes the nature of the problem. For innovation to occur we need to reward those willing to take risks and promote learning that is built on potentials and innovative thinking.

**Customer Focus** – lying in the area of close to certainty and agreement is customer *needs*. However, tension arises because flexible approaches are needed to provide them. In other words, extraordinary leadership is necessary to deliver certainty to customers. It is important to put customer goals in front of organizational or personal goals. Yet, employees are often faced with a decision 'Do I serve my customers or do I serve my organizational masters?' Organizations need to promote behaviour congruent with the messages delivered. Relationships between customers and people in organizations need to be developed at all levels (not just marketing and sales). Partnerships rather than power relationships are needed in the modern organization.

**Personal Responsibility** – Peter Block, cited on page 108, proposes that there are four core elements in a hierarchical organization:

*1. Submission to Authority* – control of our work is in the hands of those above – submission. Consequence – dependency and release from personal responsibility leading to co-dependent behaviour.

*2. Denial of Self-Expression* - denial of feelings, in turn, leads to denial of discretionary energy.

*3. Sacrifice for Unnamed Future Rewards* – a psychological contract in that sacrifice incurs obligation. That obligation used to be a secure future. In today's uncertain world this contract is violated – secure futures can't be promised.

*4. Belief That the Above are Just* - to do so promotes dependency. It says that external control is needed to focus on common goals.

Although there is some support for external control we can't ignore the probability of unpredictable events. Added to this, paradox is created in the mechanistic world - maintaining control and authority and denying self-expression drives people to fight *against* the very things they are trying to control. So in the end we don't have control at all – it is a fantasy, an illusion. The alternate belief to achieve maximum performance is that ultimate control comes from within. For many, however, the wish to maintain control is much stronger than the wish for performance. This relationship satisfies both parties - the managers who want control and the subordinates who want to avoid responsibility. Our goal is to have all members believe and act as they would if it were their own business and to take personal responsibility for how it operates.

*Extraordinary Leadership* defines success in terms of contribution and service. Managers need to offer jobs with meaning, opportunity to learn, and a chance to grow. This places a primary focus on intangible rewards with a need to be genuine, direct and definite.

**Boundaries and Guidelines** - Some rules do lie close to certainty and agreement since legislative obligations must be met. Specifically, the laws that relate to taxation, environmental parameters, industrial relations, employment, and corporate governance are examples of boundary issues. All these areas need support using mechanistic management. But some rules made from yesterday's experience may lead to dysfunctional behaviour and inappropriate responses to ever changing current issues. In these cases, instead of rules set in stone, guidelines can be developed (and renegotiated when necessary) to allow flexibility and personal judgment when faced with situations far from certainty and agreement. Shared values are the glue that holds the system together.

**Flexible Budgets to Guide** - don't let budgets rule you. Budgets are often related to negative behaviour e.g. controlling spending, rather than building business. Instead use broad plans and guiding budgets. Budgeting and planning processes are of little use with the unexpected. Also we can put a dollar value on budgets but not customer value.

**Performance Management from a Broad Base** - traditional performance management is top down. Performance management from a broad base should include customers, peers, bosses and members of the team – and not just focused on individual but include teams. Today doesn't look like yesterday, so comparisons with the past may be meaningless, as there are too many confounding variables to consider them valid or reliable. We need measures that focus on ways of achieving performance that are congruent with the values approach. Systems such as promotion based on shared knowledge not individual knowledge need to support values of broad-based performance.

In summary, we must decide whether the performance management process is individually based or team based. We must understand whether the organization is close to certainty or far from certainty and consider its impact on the performance management process. Last, we must decide the mix of qualitative and quantitative measures of performance. The choices made will impact upon the organization in its pursuit of its vision and values.

Chapter 9 provides a possible lens through which we may understand why the journey along the path of extraordinary leadership may be difficult for people.

Extraordinary leadership takes us on a journey of exciting possibilities and potentials. We have collected some case stories beginning with Chapter 10 from a variety of industries that show the potential rewards of changing the way in which we see the world of work.

# Notes

## CONSTRAINTS – SHACKLED BY BUREAUCRACY

For many years of our working lives we have struggled with an internal dilemma. We believe that most of the time almost all people want to do a good job. In fact, we can honestly say that we have met only two or three people in our entire working lives who come to work regularly to be disruptive and at times, destructive. All the anecdotal evidence suggests that this is a valid belief to hold. However, in spite of this, we have been surrounded by inefficiencies, enormous waste, industrial disputes and grievances, quality problems and poor delivery performance. Why is this so?

We believe that the fundamental cause can be traced back some 12,000 years when the first evidence of hierarchical structure can be found. In fact, it is interesting to note that the Egyptian pyramids were built using an organizational structure that was hierarchical. The main purpose of this structure was to achieve the control of large numbers of people by a few. To control large numbers of people without a hierarchical structure would result in an open-ended cylindrical structure (Figure 9.1), with every person being directly controlled by another. That is for every one-hundred workers there needs to be one hundred supervisors and for those one hundred supervisors, one hundred managers would be needed. This concept is quite bizarre.

Max Weber[84] characterized organizations into authority structures that stemmed from his basic interest in why individuals do what they are told to do. Weber distinguished between two key aspects of organization. He distinguished *power*, which is the ability to force people to obey, from *authority*, which is where orders are voluntarily obeyed. Under an authority system, people accept that orders from those in higher positions are legitimate. Weber used this platform to

---

[84] Weber, M. (1954). *Max Weber on Law in Economy and Society*, edited by Rheinstein, M. Cambridge, Mass. Harvard University Press.

develop three types of organizations but we plan to explore only one at this stage – the rational-legal model.

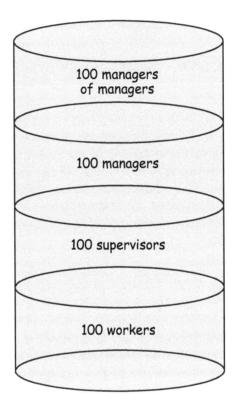

**Figure 9.1 Cylindrical Structure**

The rational legal model is bureaucratic in its basic form. This is where we create organizations that are designed to be "well-oiled machines" achieving particular targets, and every part contributes to the maximum performance of the whole system. Such organizations operate on a linear cause and effect relationship.

It is legal because power is based on rules and procedures. Precision, lack of ambiguity, knowledge of files and history, continuity, unity, strict sub-ordination, and the reduction of personal issues and cost are delivered to achieve bureaucratic efficiency.

Weber himself, uses the machine analogy. It is a structure that de-personalises the organization. In such organizations, officials occupy positions with written definitions of power limits. Those officials are arranged hierarchically and there is a set of rules and procedures to cover every foreseeable event. There is a "bureau" for the safe keeping of all written records and files. This is the rationality of the system.

For hierarchical or bureaucratic structures to exist there are two mandatory conditions. The first is *specialisation with regimentation.* If the few in control want all others to be under their control, then it is essential to limit the range of variation in available behaviours. This is similar to Weber's idea that people occupy positions that have clear limits. It is best achieved by specialisation. Not only does specialisation limit the scope of peoples' activities in a hierarchical system, but it also allows the introduction of regimentation. The aim of this is to optimise control through the reduction of variation.

The second mandatory condition is that society must share the common belief that *control is always in the level above and this is the right and proper way to organise society.*[85] It is when this belief breaks down that ordered society collapses until a new regimen can be installed. The same thing happens in our businesses and other types of organization. Although the breakdown may not be a complete overthrow of those in power, it expresses itself in much more subtle forms in organizational life. The "annual restructuring" of the organization is an obvious example. We shall pursue this later in much more detail.

**So what?**

As demonstrated above, these essential platforms,

1) specialisation with regimentation, and
2) the shared belief that control is always in the level above

have the following impacts on hierarchical structures (Figure 9.2)

---

[85] Dick.R., *"Creating the learning organization"*, prepared for a workshop for the Australian Public Service Commission, Canberra, November 1993.

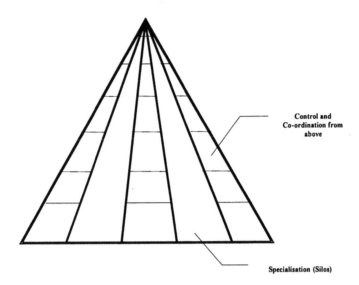

Control and
Co-ordination from
above

Specialisation (Silos)

**Figure 9.2 Specialisation "silos" and Control From Above**

The impact of specialisation is to create "silos" within the organization. These obviously restrict the extent of horizontal movement by creating powerful and clearly defined rigid boundaries. The objective here is to achieve control by limiting the scope of work. Specialisation meant that work was broken down into simple tasks and distributed to a number of people. This thinking is most obvious in the work of the economist Adam Smith and implemented masterfully by Henry Ford, founder of the Ford Motor Company, as well in the Taylorist model we talk about in PATOP.

Every day we see examples of control and restrictions in action. In industrial settings there are clear boundaries between what the operators of plant and equipment do and those who maintain that plant. Similarly, there are clear boundaries between those responsible for the supply of materials and services to the production process, those responsible for the management of people services, those who do the marketing and those involved in research and development, to name just a few. We are sure that the reader can produce what seems to be an infinite list of examples.

The effect of coordination and control in the level above causes vertical barriers in our hierarchical structures. Here the worker does the work and the boss, at all levels in the system does the planning and coordinating. You may recall that it was no more than 10 to 15 years ago that you would have found yourself in a management development program learning the 4 principles of management. The principles were planning, organising, directing, and controlling. This had the impact of reinforcing the hierarchical differences between those who do the work and those involved in the planning, coordinating and controlling of the work. It also reinforced the elitist nature of management and downgraded the value of work done at levels below management. This can be clearly seen in industrial practice where the division of labour (influenced by the writings of Adam Smith and later by Frederick Taylor)[86] breaks tasks down to simple activities that often mimic machine behaviour.

We would now like to explore the impact of these barriers in a real life situation. Let us imagine that we are operating in an industrial environment and that the production process is no longer performing to specification. The first person to see the problem is an operator of the plant or a repairer of the plant. Because of the belief around planning and coordinating being in the level above they are unable to take action to fix the problem. Instead they are obliged to pass the information to the person who is at the next level in the hierarchy. That person considers the situation, and again applies the rule that "the control and coordination is in the level above" and passes it to the next level. That person reviews the information available, and again passes it to the level above. Conceptually the CEO would make all of the day-to-day decisions in this scenario. But we know that organizations cannot operate that way. So we put in some "circuit breakers", such as delegated power to supervisors and managers that define decision points in our hierarchical structure.

As the information travels its way up the hierarchical structure it suffers from a loss of integrity. The quality of the information becomes both consciously and unconsciously distorted. Each person reviewing the information and preparing it for transmission to the next level, sees it through the filters of his or her past experience and changes it accordingly.

The information and perception of the decision-maker may also be influenced by the physical position that the person takes in relation

---

[86] Taylor, F.W. (1947) *Scientific Management, New York.* Harper & Row.

to the problem. Imagine that you had a group of people sitting in a circle in a room and you asked the people sitting in the northern, southern, eastern and western positions to describe the room as they looked directly ahead. The descriptions would vary significantly and, if the listener did not have any experience of the room, he or she would conclude that they were describing different rooms. Therefore, our physical position in relation to the event will influence our perceptions.

There is a further possibility, and that is, people consciously distort information in order to protect themselves. Often they wish to prove that they are not responsible if something goes wrong, or that the system, which they manage, is not out of control. This is called lying. Lying often leads to blame, fear and mistrust. This in turn leads to negative political behaviour throughout the whole organization.

The third problem with the transmission of information is that the intangible or tacit information is lost. In a hierarchical system only the tangible facts and data are valued and the intangible information around feelings, beliefs and intuitive judgments are not considered legitimate. How many times has any one of us had a really strong sense that the equipment that we are operating is not functioning properly but we don't know why? Likely, when we take it to our boss and suggest that it is not operating correctly, we are told to come back with some facts and data.

This last point is illustrated very clearly in the banking system. Usually applicants who are seeking substantial loans have their applications taken to a "credit committee" within the bank. Those committees usually comprise the banks' senior executives. Prior to reaching the credit committee, each proposal goes through a number of levels in the hierarchy where much of the subjective information is eliminated before it actually arrives at the credit committee.

Why does this happen? We think it is the result of the desire for safety by those charged with making the decisions on the applications for loans. After all, the decision-makers can't be held responsible where the decisions are supported by facts and data – 'black numbers, printed numbers on white paper'.

There are other subjective pieces of information crucial to effective decision making that are totally lost in the process because subjectivity is considered both unsafe and requires personal accountability. This is a clear example of a senior group in an organization attempting to exercise control in an environment where the integrity of the data must be incomplete or suspect because of the data that is rejected. The irony is that the incomplete information raises the risk factor and generates an even greater desire for safety.

The other major problem with information flowing up the chain of command is that it takes time and consumes resources that inflict an unnecessary cost on the organization, resulting in lost opportunities. In the production example we mentioned earlier, the process continues to produce product that may well be outside the customer specification thereby generating waste. The lack of involvement also produces complacency in workers, since they rarely get feedback or responses when really needed. They often just give up. They believe that if those in positions above theirs don't care, why should they?

Under such circumstances as both the hierarchical production process and the bank credit committee process, one would expect that the decision-makers would have only a 50/50 chance of making a decision that is in the best interest of the business. However in reality we find that this is, say, closer to 70% or more, of the decisions being in the best interest of the business.

This means that 30% or less, of the decisions that are made are obviously not in the best interest of the business. (These figures are guesses based on the authors' experiences and limited anecdotal evidence and are used only to illustrate the point being made within a more realistic frame.) Now lets trace the 30%. A decision is made at the top. The decision is repeatedly delivered to the level below. Each time it passes through the levels below it gets distorted and reinterpreted until finally it reaches the bottom of the system where action needs to be taken. Upon hearing the decision, the person usually replies that 'only an idiot manager could make a decision like that. If only s/he could get out of his/her ivory tower...doesn't s/he care about the business... don't they care about the customers...don't managers care about my job?"

At this point we would like to take you back to our starting point, and that is we believe that almost all people come to work and want to do a good job most of the time. So we assume that the manager who made the decision actually comes to work and wants to do a good job. She doesn't want to deliberately disrupt the work place by taking inappropriate actions to deal with problems. Rather she wants to go home and feel that she has had an opportunity to work with pride and has contributed positively to the organization. Similarly, employees at the bottom of the hierarchical system would like to do the same.

Although a scenario from heavy industry has been used here, the same actions and resulting feelings exist with shop assistants, airline staff, customer service officers in banks, etc. In fact, those people who have the greatest contact with the organization's customers or who add direct value to the organization's processes may feel the impact of inappropriate decisions rapidly and more strongly. The symbolic message of lack of care is reinforced. (Later we will talk about the 'shadow system' or 'counter-culture' and what we are describing here are the first steps along that path).

An interesting observation is how we all go along with such arrangements. We may instinctively know that we are colluding in maintaining a hierarchical system that fosters sub-optimal performance. Put simply, we support a system that sets each of us to fail. The hierarchical system fails to perform because it distorts the information essential to effective decision-making. Information is crucial to extraordinary organizational performance and the creation of wealth.

Although the above comments are critical, it should be remembered that such systems have provided society with enormous material benefits. That is not to say that perhaps even greater benefits could have been available to employees and shareholders. We speak with the benefit of hindsight.

It was probably up until World War Two that the hierarchical system remained unchallenged. Our fantasy was that people had made enormous sacrifices during the war years and were no longer willing to accept the goods and services that were previously provided. They wanted houses that they could design, white goods, motor vehicles with a range of options, entertainment, and a raft of goods and services denied them during the war years.

The hierarchical system that was asked to meet these new demands was largely incapable of doing so without modification. One of the modifications to achieve the flexibility required, was to employ more people.

At this point it might be useful to mention that a hierarchical system is set up to achieve three significant outcomes. They are stability, certainty and predictability. In fact, there is probably no better way of ensuring that tomorrow will look like yesterday than managing our processes in a bureaucratic or hierarchical way. This is the first major point of tension. On the one hand, people are demanding flexible and adaptable responses from the organizations established to serve their needs. On the other hand, those organizations from which they are seeking adaptability and responsiveness, are built to deliver the very opposite - stability, certainty and predictability.

The dilemma was and probably still is, how to build flexibility into processes that were designed for stability. An initial approach was to put extra people in the production and service processes with the view to giving the organization flexibility. These spare resources or 'redundant parts'[87] were developed to enable the system to respond flexibly to changing requirements. For example, in the early 1970's, the number of employees that BHP Ltd (a large Australian mining, energy and steel manufacturing company) had at its steel works at Port Kembla (some 80 km south of Sydney) was somewhere in the order of 24,000. In 2002, we believe that the figure is less than one quarter of that number. Why so many in the 1960's? Apart from some "featherbedding" that creeps into most large organizations over time, and more reliance on labour intensive processes of production, a factor was that extra people were needed to give this organization flexibility to respond to the changing requirements of customers. Fred Emery calls this 'redundancy of parts."[88]

[87] Emery, M. (editor) (1993) Participative Design for Participative Democracy, Canberra. Centre for Continuing Education, Australian National University
[88] Emery, F. (1989) The Light on the Hill, in M. Emery. Ed. Participative Design for Participative Democracy . Canberra. Centre for Continuing Education Australian National University, (p 102)

If you look at a piano you will see that it has 88 notes, which can play almost every piece of music written, but at any point of time most of the notes are redundant to immediate requirements. They exist to give the piano flexibility. Similarly, "redundant" parts existed in organizations to give them flexibility.

Why not put more people in so that there is always someone to attend to things that crop up? That's exactly what happened, but of course, if nothing cropped up, s/he became a redundant part.

What was totally missed (apart from Fred Emery[88] who developed the theory of redundant parts and redundant functions which is in the PATOP chapter) was recognition and appreciation of the flexibility present in every worker, given the conditions under which s/he can or will exercise it. Just as 88 notes on a piano can give endless varieties of music, skills and capabilities of human beings can be drawn upon when needed. In other words, we have many facets of ourselves that we use (and do not use) at any given time. Continuing the metaphor, this suggests that what we are seeking are "violin" type organizations rather than the "piano" type – where at any point of time all four strings of the violin are in use, with each string having redundant notes. In organizations, people are engaged in productive activities at any point of time but some of the competencies that they posses are not being used at a particular point of time. Emery called this the theory of redundant functions.

In 1987 a significant event occurred in Australia and throughout the world that led to greater pressures being applied to organizations. The "stock market crash" of October 1987, reshaped many organizations. The response to that "crash" was to do what had always been done in times of crisis – cut costs! So we systematically went about 'downsizing' and invoking other cost reduction campaigns. The impact was to reduce the flexibility of organizations. It created increased stress within organizations because the previous rigid control systems remained in place but extra people did not. In other words, when a worker was absent, or when an unexpected demand was delivered, there was no one available.

This 'shell shocked' state continued to exist through the late nineteen-eighties and early nineties when organizations began to discover 'Total Quality Management' or TQM. TQM presented the leaders of our organizations with a new challenge. The challenge was to create organizations that were *adaptable, flexible and customer focused*. As you can quickly see this is the antithesis of the outputs of bureaucratic organizations. This created tension between what was said and actively promoted throughout organizations and the actions and behaviours observed. Argyris and Schön[89] refer to this as the tension between "espoused theories" and "theories in use'. In the end, people pay attention to what they see or the behaviours adopted rather than the words that they hear. In bureaucracies, people model their behaviour on what they see happening above.

Still the quest for how to get flexibility from systems designed to produce stability continued. To find *the solution* many experiments were undertaken. We spent our time looking for the one right answer or the formula, which would provide a solution. Many organizations decided that the Japanese had models that would provide the answers. In particular, the Japanese strategies for involvement through quality circles attracted our attention. Quality circles appeared widely throughout industry and government under many names such as, "business improvement teams", "process improvement teams", and so on.

Our experience suggests that these had a time span of between 9 and 12 months before they became irrelevant. In the first two months of their existence, those improvement teams often achieved quite stunning results because they were able to address obvious inefficiencies in the systems. They had been given the legitimacy and the right to "fix the work place". As resources continued to be applied to the quality circles the law of diminishing returns began to operate. The gains from the regular injection of resources were beginning to diminish. In rugby football, you would say initially that they were taking "the easy yards". They were able to address obvious problems that had plagued the organizations in which the quality circles were introduced. However, as the system moves closer towards its capacity, the opportunities for improvement rapidly diminish. Here the law of diminishing returns operates. For the same unit of investment, the returns begin to fall. As we get close to maximum performance, our capacity to generate the same level of improvement is not possible.

[89] Argyris, C & Schön, D. (1978) *Organizational Learning: A Theory of Action Perspective.* Reading, Mass, Addison-Wesley.

Evangelists of quality circles often argued that the world seemed to be governed by straight lines or normal distribution. The relationship between inputs and outputs was certainly not a straight-line positive relationship. In fact, it probably looks more like the following diagram (Figure 9.3).

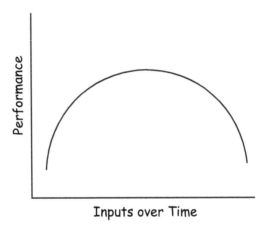

Inputs over Time

**Figure 9.3 The Life Cycle of Quality Improvement Teams**

At low levels of performance, it can be illustrated that, an investment in improvement team activities generates a significant increase in performance. However, as we get closer to the top of the curve we can see that the same increase in inputs results in a very small improvement in performance. Beyond the top point of the curve, continuing investment actually leads to a drop in performance.

Eventually, support for those types of interventions diminishes to the point where they disappear. Lets pause and consider this situation. You will have guessed that there is some problem in 'measuring' quality circles by outcomes and demonstrable solutions. It is only OK to engage workers' brains on tangible problems. Once these are resolved, it is time to put the brains back in the box because the valuable resources given to quality teams are needed elsewhere.

This is particularly so where the quality circles start to compete with the functional "silos" for resources and are seen to distract people from the perceived 'real work' of the silos. Managers start complaining that production and service levels are declining because people are being distracted from their day-to-day work by being involved in long-term improvement activities. In addition, we start to see decision-making by "rent-a-crowd". This refers to the situations that arise where decisions that were previously undertaken by one or two competent people, are now being taken by large groups of perhaps not so expert people. There is a consequent negative impact on production and service levels. Managers fight to maintain production and service levels and reduce the cost structures of their "silos" by starving the quality circles of resources.

As the perceived usefulness of the quality circles diminished, a search began for the next stage in the development of our organizations.

To counteract the loss of integrity of information as it passed up and down the bureaucratic process and to reduce the delays in responding to problems, it seemed that the logical conclusion was to give those closest to the points of action the power to make decisions. A new idea, "empowerment" was given birth. This makes a great deal of sense as an objective. However, the history of implementation has been disappointing.

Many managers embraced this new idea with enthusiasm and often delivered edicts demanding that this be the new reform for their organizations. As a result many work teams at the 'value-adding end' of the business were suddenly asked to make decisions for which they were ill prepared. Nor did this have the support of the middle managers who saw danger and loss of job security in the empowerment strategies.

Logically, however, if one expects the same level of decision making that occurs further up the hierarchy, then four crucial factors need to be put in place. The first is, that those people being asked to make the decisions need the same **technical competency** as those in more senior positions.

> **Four crucial factors need to be put in place – the first is, that those people being asked to make the decisions need the same level of technical competency as those in more senior positions.**

James Champy[90] points to managers who thought that empowering workers meant disempowering themselves. "They didn't give an inch, keeping the power to make decisions to themselves, yet talking fluently about empowerment".

Technical competency requires some clarification at this point. Often technical competency is understood to be the development of manuals and procedures that tell people who carry out defined tasks, what to do. At times this is complemented by some problem-solving built around taught solutions. What is usually missing when solutions are presented, is a full explanation of the processes being worked upon with an emphasis on understanding it from first principles. Understanding from first principles is where the science that underpins the process of manufacture or service is understood. This is what we consider to be technical competency – where the person working on the process can develop creative, innovative and unique solutions to the situations encountered. It takes the work from "black magic" and "art", to "science".

> **The second fundamental piece of infrastructure needed is the development of social competency.**

The second fundamental piece of infrastructure needed is the development of social competency. People must be proficient in those skills necessary to maintain relationships within the team of which they are a part. This is as well as maintaining relationships with other significant people and other teams within the system. Each person must have the ability to influence others in the system in order to secure support and gain information that is necessary for quality decision making to occur.

The third vital piece of infrastructure is access to information. If a consistent level of decision-making is required throughout the organization, then each decision-maker must have the same access to information.

---

[90] Champy, J. (1995). *Reengineering management: The mandate for new leadership.* London, Harper Collins.

> ## The third vital piece of infrastructure is access to information.

The information that is traditionally held at senior levels now has to be distributed more widely. To restrict its distribution guarantees sub-optimal decision-making and performance. The implications for the formal and informal information systems are enormous. The ability to effectively collect, analyse and disseminate information is what differentiates high performing organizations from others.

The <u>fourth</u> piece of infrastructure is perhaps the most difficult to achieve. It is to give people "freedom to act".

Many readers will be surprised and some even offended by this suggestion. "What do you mean? I give people freedom to act!" you might be thinking. But do you?

> **The fourth piece of infrastructure is perhaps the most difficult to achieve. It is to give people "freedom to act".**

Freedom to act is about creating a safe environment where people can feel secure in making decisions. It is an environment where people feel supported if the decisions made yield unexpected outcomes. It is a learning environment where people usually accept that there are no mistakes, just unexpected outcomes. The only time that people will be punished in this system is if they do something illegal, act in a way that is contrary to understood and agreed procedures, or there is a proven case of personal negligence and not just systemic variation. Otherwise, they can expect and will receive absolute backing for the decisions made.

It is about creating a culture that is not focused on blame. Rather, it is a culture focused on learning.

> **It is about creating a culture that is not focused on blame. Rather, it is a culture focused on learning.**

There are many examples of organizations increasing the technical and social competency of their employees and providing all employees with access to the information needed to make decisions that are in the best interests of the organization. However, there are few examples of organizations that provide genuine freedom to act. Why?

Well, the rational side of all of us understands the need to do so. However, to give people freedom to act in a bureaucratic system challenges one of the fundamental pillars that support the hierarchical structure – that is, *"control and co-ordination is always in the level above"*.

This is a conflict between "head" (delegate authority) and "heart" (retain power over decision making) and the well-ingrained beliefs override more rational processes. It results in conflicting signals being delivered within the organization. Under these circumstances, people actually pay attention to and trust what they see (i.e. the actions and behaviors) rather than what they hear. The result is that we have a culture where there is dissonance between what people say they will do and what is actually done.

Because of this dissonance and the fundamental belief that control and co-ordination rests in the level above, such structures become obsessed with *accountability*. The driver of the obsession is the fact that such systems present the most elaborate ways of avoiding personal responsibility. If we collude in maintaining the belief that control and co-ordination are legitimately held in the level above, we do not have to take responsibility for the results of our actions. After all, the boss owns the system that we work in.

POWER

**Figure 9.4 Power Running Down the Organization**

Because power runs down the hierarchical system, people are drawn to look up (Figure 9.4). To talk about paying attention to forces outside the organization, such as customers, becomes nonsense when the internal requirements of maintaining rules is in conflict with satisfying customers. In most cases, the politically smart move is to play the hierarchical game. After all, it is the boss that determines pay levels, job security, overtime, training opportunities, etc. The desire for stability, certainty, and predictability can only be found by looking inwards and upwards in a hierarchical structure. This becomes seductive. The alternative is to look outwards, where customers are living with unpredictability and change as their currency.

The tension in the system is about honouring those beautifully printed and framed statements that are strategically placed around our organizations. They demand that we be customer focused, flexible and adaptable, whist all the behaviours and actions within the system tell us to stick to the rules and deliver certainty, predictability and stability and most of all, behave politically by "playing the game."

If these structures are no longer useful, then what do we replace them with? This presents a set of major issues. The _first_ is that we are trying to look for new solutions through hierarchical lenses. Einstein once said that no problem can be solved from the same thinking that created it. The _second_ problem is an assumption that there is one best model. In situations of high complexity (which in reality, reflects the world we live in) the search for a single model or formula is not at all useful. The _third_ problem is that we are not sure that we have the courage to throw out the current systems and start with a blank sheet. Even if we had the courage, would we run the risk of merely replacing one set of known problems for another set of yet unknown problems? The search for new ways of being together is essential, particularly as information technology challenges every operation within society. We need to look for new ways to "dance" with the environment.

What does dancing with the environment mean? To us it means moving together in time to the tune, adapting to each other's movements. It may mean compensating for unexpected changes in tempo and then finding the stability of the time and tune once more. In other words, it is about interacting in a stable yet constantly evolving way, at one time preserving and at another transforming basic steps into something unique. It is the quality of the transformation that has led organizational writers such as Ralph D Stacey[91] and Margaret J Wheatley[92], to pose provocative, yet intuitively appealing questions about the way we organize.

---

[91] Stacey, R.D. (1996) _Strategic Management & Organizational Dynamics 2nd Ed._ London, Pitman.
[92] Wheatley, M .J. (1994) _Leadership and the New Science: Learning about Organization from an Orderly Universe._ San Francisco, Berrett-Koehler.

# Chapter 10

## Introduction to Stories
## — "The World of Experiences"

The stories we present here are no ordinary ones. They tell of ideas such as the ones we have shared throughout the book being put into practice. How hard is it do you think, to change from the mechanistic environment to the extraordinary one? Given the subtle ways that control is applied, now that it is politically incorrect to be seen to command and control people, we would say that it is very difficult indeed. Yet the people who have generously contributed their stories fall into this category. We hope that you enjoy them as we tell them in historical order and with great appreciation to the authors.

### 1. Dalrymple Bay Coal Terminal

Andrew Carter provides an honest and deeply reflective account of the Terminal's journey. He talks about beginning the process with a typical planning approach and as people gain confidence, challenging their understanding of the planning process. It is interesting to observe how various issues and questions emerged, and how the organization chose to respond to those emerging issues.

It is a true example of an organization that has increased its performance by concentrating on the development of its intangible assets. The focus on the intangible assets has been largely responsible for the stunning growth in the performance of the Terminal (ie. from 26mtpa to 55mtpa in a just few years). It is clear that developing trusting relationships and a strong sense of identity has resulted in timely and comprehensive information flows within the operation. The quality and timeliness of information, together with the release of the discretionary energy of people, has contributed to the Terminal's performance. Alma recently interviewed many of the people at Dalrymple Bay (hard hat, steel boots and on the night shift)

and it was an amazing experience to hear people in this coal-encrusted environment talking about 'the good of the business', 'our team values', 'when there are issues, we bring them to the team as people are fragile and we do not want anyone to suffer' (actual quotes). There was absolutely no doubt that the business was everyone's business and whatever had to be done to keep 'simply the best' would be done.

### 2. Mineral International
(A pseudonym to protect the organization's identity)

This story is about a client organization that David has worked with over a number of years. It tells a story of the tensions that are often experienced in challenging the paradigms held by key members of an organization. It is probably representative of the experiences of many as they challenge the fantasy that organizations live in a world of certainty and, that absolute predictability is possible.

A fundamental piece in this story is the acceptance that there is a legitimate need to develop a responsive capacity as well as the capacity to predict. Extraordinary performance can only be achieved when both capacities are developed within the organization.

### 3. The Whyalla Rolling Mills

Geoff Voigt's "Whyalla story" from 1999 captures his journey to that date. The Whyalla experience was initiated by the application of a socio-technical approach to organization change. Initially, it was not possible during that period to introduce to some the ideas included in this book because the organization had not reached a level of understanding that would have gained acceptance of those concepts. Secondly, we as consultants, had rather crude conceptual frameworks and limited practical experience of the application of the model of Extraordinary Leadership. Geoff's story probably represents a significant step in his company's journey of understanding organizations as places of complexity and adaptation rather than mechanistic creations.

However, it was interesting to observe how the process worked and how new opportunities constantly emerged. The people involved often displayed surprise at what was achieved and were in frequent conversation about how it felt to challenge the existing management paradigms by taking themselves to the edge of chaos.

### 4. The Metropolitan Cemeteries Board

The Metropolitan Cemeteries Board is a statutory authority, established by the government of Western Australia. Its Chief Executive Officer, Peter MacLean tells of his organization's journey over a number of years with a particular emphasis on building an organization that is values based. It is interesting to reflect on the organization's handling of external pressures and the paradox's it faced in exercising extraordinary leadership.

Some of the features of the Metropolitan Cemeteries Board story are the importance of information in achieving outstanding performance, and the relationship between information, trusting relationships and identity. A second feature is the customer focus and the potential tension between it and the requirements of the bureaucratic functions.

What is not mentioned in the story, are the many innovations that have emerged from the cultural changes but trust us, there were many. One for example, was the development of an electronic site that celebrated the life of the deceased person, as well as the funeral. This allowed access to the funeral and whatever was stored electronically, for those distant friends and relatives.

# Notes

## COMPLEX ADAPTIVE SYSTEMS IN PRACTICE AT DALRYMPLE BAY COAL TERMINAL (DBCT)

### Dr Andrew C Carter, CEO, 2003

Thirty-eight kilometres south of the central Queensland City of Mackay is Hay Point. The Cumberland Islands, 2km offshore the southern most islands of Queensland's popular Whitsunday's, provide an idyllic seascape when viewed from the once tranquil coastal communities of Half Tide and Louisa Creek. Hay Point is now home to one of Australia's largest ports and the site of Dalrymple Bay Coal Terminal, Queensland's fastest growing coal export facility – throughput has risen from 26 million tonnes per annum (mtpa) in 1998 through to 40mtpa in 2001, and has kept improving to date.

Since its inception in 1981 (first coal was shipped in 1983) the Terminal has experienced unprecedented growth. This growth is set to be maintained with 60mtpa throughput capacity being planned for post 2005.

The Terminal, a unique partnership between the State Government of Queensland and four farsighted coal-mining companies, has undergone numerous stages of development and metamorphism during the last 20 years.

The Terminal's operation, initially under a Management Agreement, and more recently under the provisions of an Operating and Maintenance Contract (OMC), was an innovative arrangement permitting users of the Terminal to own the Terminal management company, whilst the State facilitated the development of Bowen Basin export coal mines via the provision of Terminal expansion capital.

The initial four coal-mining companies have now been joined by five others and the State Government's interest has recently passed from the hands of the Port's Corporation of Queensland (a State Government corporation), under long term lease, to an investor consortium led by Babcock and Brown; Coal Logistics North Queensland.

Dalrymple Bay Coal Terminal Pty Ltd (DBCT P/L) was formed in 1981 to manage, operate and maintain the Terminal. From the outset, operations were scheduled 24 hours per day, seven days per week, 365 days per year. With operations spread over six kilometres, some unique challenges were faced from day one of operations and a strong focus was placed on both the recognition of the range of skills assembled during the recruitment of DBCT P/L employees and the achievements of its people. It was into this environment that a new CEO and General Manager, Dr Andrew Carter, was appointed in June 1997 to take over from the retiring CEO.

His was a hard act to follow – Captain Denis Holden, the foundation CEO, was a master mariner of many years standing having gone to sea at the age of 15 years old. In 1965 he pioneered the establishment of the Pilbara iron ore industry via the development of the Port of Dampier. From 1965 up to the time of his appointment with DBCT P/L, the Port of Dampier was transformed from a remote and uninhabited island into Australia's largest port, exporting some 60 million tonnes of iron ore, salt and LNG.

I confessed during my early meetings with DBCT P/L personnel, 'What I know about running a Terminal you can write on the head of a pin. That is your role - mine is to seek to tap that experience and maximise your contribution to the future success of this organization'. These are reflections of that journey.

The initial reaction reflected the undoubted pride and sense of achievement that pervaded the organization. The achievements in establishing the Terminal, its subsequent operation and expansion during testing times, both technical and natural, were coupled with an appreciation of the natural environment of the area and the lifestyle offered. The successful operation of a coal terminal adjacent to the Great Barrier Reef Marine Park was in itself a noteworthy achievement.

The sense of 'ownership' was both a positive and a negative. A brief glimpse into the future with the advent of National Competition Policy and the imminent expiry of the Management Agreement with

PCQ (Ports Corporation Queensland) meant that that DBCT P/L people had to come to grips with the fact that, although instrumental in the success of the Terminal, they were not part of the Terminal fabric. It was the skills that they brought and the intellect that they applied to both manage the expectations of the Terminal's customers and subsequently deliver on those expectations which would determine the future success of DBCT P/L.

The 'can do' attitude, and the recognition that a balance could be struck between the future success of the business and lifestyle offered, provided reassurance that the expectations of the Board of DBCT P/L were achievable.

The early priorities were therefore emerging as:

- The need to understand the implications of the future and articulate the organizational goals;
- The need for the guiding members of the organization to exhibit behaviours consistent with the achievement of the organization's stated goals and
- The need to tap into and develop the undoubted willingness of DBCT P/L's people to maximise their contribution to the achievement of the organization's goals.

There would also be hard decisions to be made: Terminal expansion continued unabated, the complexity of the operation was about to rise exponentially, and the nature of the export coal market was changing markedly from that envisaged at the time of the Terminal's inception.

It is worthwhile noting that experience had tempered the expectations of a change process which sought to achieve change solely on the basis of understanding or intellectual challenge.

Willingness or, as I will later refer to, discretionary energy, was going to be a key component in the achievement of DBCT P/L goals. Given the close linkages between work, success at work – be it increasing capacity, community perception or managing the environment – and lifestyle, that same experience indicated that an underlying value structure existed which could be tapped into to release this discretionary energy.

The intellectual challenge for the guiding members of DBCT P/L was addressed via the development of an 'applied strategic planning process'. The objective of the process was to permit the guiding members of the organization to envision the company's future and develop the necessary procedures and operations to achieve that future. The envisioning process created the belief that aspects of the future can be influenced and changed by what one does now.

The applied strategic planning process developed focussed on the 'process of planning', not the plan produced.

The challenge for the Executive Management Team (EMT) was to:

- accept that they were assuming the mantle of being the guiding members of the organization;
- accept accountability for the fact that what they did would influence, both positively and negatively, the future of the organization and
- recognise that the changing world would require the application of the skills and learning from the past, in a very different environment.

Focussing on the process and not the plan, represented a subtle shift from other planning processes in that compliance was not an acceptable behaviour - genuine commitment or ownership was the only logical outcome. (I will refer to some of the tensions that emerged with the EMT when this focus was lost during one phase of our journey.)

Members of the EMT recognised that genuine commitment would visit areas that many of them had never explored. Having commenced the process, time was spent with the EMT to permit them to commence their exploration. The group decided that self-knowledge would assist and time was spent in seeking to understand team development and team performance by sharing individual data.

There were EMT casualties resulting from the personal challenges faced during the development and implementation of the applied strategic planning process adopted. The openness within which the process evolved permitted senior personnel to exit DBCT P/L with dignity.

It is interesting to note that at the commencement of the planning process there appeared to be a genuine expectation that the EMT would return from a workshop and issue a 'Notice to Employees' explaining what they had done.

As can be interpreted from the stated challenges for the EMT, these were difficult and confusing times – not likely to be resolved by a 'road to Damascus' experience. The EMT did not have a clear picture of the future.

The envisioning process resulted in the development of EMT Operating Principles which were ultimately shared with the rest of the organization, not with a view to gaining their acceptance but as an overt statement of the espoused beliefs by which actions of the EMT could be judged.

The alignment of the EMT Operating Principles, with the environmental scan undertaken of DBCT P/L peoples' perceptions of what was good, what was bad and what could be done better, was not unexpected. The maturity of the EMT in both developing the process and pursuing the process to develop Operating Principles demonstrated the correctness of focussing on the 'process of planning'.

As in all change processes there is no one correct way. External pressures were mounting with the need for additional throughput in an environment of increasing operational complexity.

The need to test and tap into the organizational willingness/ discretionary energy was emerging as a critical change issue.

The physical design of the facility at Dalrymple Bay Coal Terminal lends itself to high levels of consistency and repeatability in operation. Feeders, conveyor belts, stackers, reclaimers, stacker/reclaimers, ship loaders have design rates and an inherent ability to be operated with certainty and agreement. If one defines 'normal management' as operating in areas close to certainty and close to agreement, it could be argued that engineering had been successfully used to eliminate uncertainty from the operation of the Terminal.

This could not be further from the truth in that the supply chain, of which the Terminal is one component, exhibits significant variability due to both natural and supply chain system events.

The combination of these unpredictable supply chain events often results in terminal operations approaching the 'edge of chaos'. This is not to imply that the Terminal is out of control with the prospect of imminent harm to people, product, assets and the environment. In essence, for terminal operations to sustain its ability to manage the complexity of the interaction of the many systems converging on the Terminal, 'normal management' needs to be supplemented by what could be best described as 'extraordinary leadership' – the world of relationships, trust, information – which would only be realised by tapping into DBCT P/L's discretionary energy.

The congruency between the need to sustain the operation of the Terminal 'at the edge of chaos' through the application of the principles of both 'normal management' and 'extraordinary leadership' and the EMT's envisioned future of DBCT P/L was compelling.

DBCT P/L's envisioned future saw it assuming a key strategic role with respect to the management of the coal chain. This role, a logical assumption once the coal supply chain was viewed as an integrated activity within which Terminal out loading – ship loading – is the system bottleneck, was to be undertaken without the benefit of contractual arrangements and in the full knowledge of the vagaries of shipping and the impact of weather on both mine production capacity and each element of the supply chain.

Knowledge management was an emerging pre-requisite for the future success of DBCT P/L.

Relationships, trust, the use of information, a desire driven by discretionary energy to test limits, were all facets of the envisioned future for DBCT P/L which would seek to differentiate it from its competitors.

Equally importantly, the knowledge of process, the use of systems, the ability to apply and benefits of Normal Management would underpin both DBCT P/L's credibility and community acceptance of its licence to operate.

Experiential learning, permitting both exposure to and recognition of the power of operating in a world of Extraordinary leadership was seen as a critical part of the journey for both the EMT and those within the organization who were clearly puzzled by the disappearance of some of the more classic features of command and control management. Not only were the classic features of command and control management disappearing, the exhibited behaviour was totally consistent with the espoused Operating Principles of the EMT, including that of, 'doing what you say you are going to do.'

Access to this experiential learning by the EMT and a broad cross section of DBCT P/L people provided a further insight, albeit not clearly, into the envisioned future of the organization.

In many respects what we sought to create or solve, was the assembly of a jigsaw puzzle without having a clear understanding of the picture, in DBCT P/L's case – the future. Envisioning the future, I would like to think, gave us the ability to complete much of the outside – the straight pieces. The inside was much more complex with an ability to assemble small patches of colour but we were unsure as to their precise location within the boundary of the straight pieces – or in fact whether they were even part of the final picture. It could be said that we are assembling patches of colour based on experience and historical paradigms when neither are necessarily part of the future.

To do a jigsaw puzzle you need both the intellectual understanding – the head stuff – and the discretionary energy to persevere – the heart stuff.

An additional level of complexity is introduced by operating in today's society, in that where previously many organizations believed that, once established, they had an almost 'God given' right to exist, society today, correctly, continuously re-assesses the balance between wealth creation and consumption of resources such that even the straight pieces on the outside of the jigsaw puzzle are subject to change.

In DBCT P/L's case, we did not know what the detail of picture looked like. The patches of colour we created were subject to change based on future experience. The straight pieces on the outside, on which we thought we might have been able to hang the patches of colour, were also subject to change.

A phrase coined by our people at this time was 'Managers in the Mist'. It provided an insight as to how, as an EMT, we were operating close to the edge of chaos. Whether it recognised acceptance of the need for the organization to operate in an environment of uncertainty was hard to conclude.

Reflection on process is always valuable and during one of those EMT reflective periods, it was apparent that despite the promulgation of the EMT's Operating Principles and experiential learning opportunities, there remained more than healthy scepticism between the reality and DBCT P/L's envisioned future.

There remained both history and slime.

The honouring of history became an important part of our journey now and, as both the rate and scale of change accelerated, in the future.

The slime existed under a number of rocks that had remained untouched for many years. Despite the EMT operating principle of 'address the hard issues', it was apparent that rocks, not known to the EMT, needed to be found, lifted and the slime exposed and expunged.

The slime encompassed both organizational sins of the past, and tolerated behaviours which were inconsistent both with respect to EMT operating principles and what people had seen as being valuable from the experiential learning.

As can be seen from the above, the analogy to the jigsaw puzzle becomes more apparent, in that to the casual observer moving from experiential learning to slime removal seems illogical. However it provides insights into the ultimate vision and the need to create patches of colour as and when they are perceived.

There will always be periods in the future when uncertainty, or mist, will be present. In essence this uncertainty, when occurring within an organization which has come to realise that uncertainty is a truer reflection of real life than certainty, provides both energy and hence life to the organization.

The EMT and others were operating close to the edge of chaos. The principles of 'extraordinary leadership' were being applied and significant personal and organizational growth was occurring.

The ability to concentrate on those areas in clear focus and in a manner consistent with the EMT's stated Operating Principles continued to advance the organization's objectives since those key behaviours provided consistency and reinforced the envisioned future of the organization.

It is also interesting to note the tensions within the EMT concerning Critical Success Indicators (CSI's). These tensions and the need for CSI's indicated the difficulty of the almost continuous change process which the organization was experiencing and the resulting difficulty in determining what DBCT P/L was.

As noted earlier, the transition from a Management Agreement to an Operating and Maintenance Contract (OMC) had caused a rude awakening in that DBCT P/L people were not part of the fabric of the Terminal.

The CSI's, under the Management Agreement, which permitted the tolling of coal through the Terminal had been tonnes and nett cost. Nett cost included as a revenue item income derived from associated Terminal towage operations. Was DBCT P/L therefore a successful terminal operator with access to a well-run towage business; or a towage operator who happened to be managing a terminal? Under the OMC, it could be argued that profit was a 'contractor objective'. The OMC did however limit profit to 10% of direct costs – costs which the DBCT P/L Board wanted minimised, thus eroding profit.

Over a three-year period these tensions remained unresolved. Each time CSI's were raised a consensus around certain aspects of the business was emerging. A common theme was 'harm' – the avoidance of harm to:

- our people
- our customer's product,
- our client's equipment, and
- the environment.

In parallel with the development of this CSI, was the emergence of the realisation that DBCT P/L was truly a 'management service provider'. Whilst avoiding the emotive and unsustainable words such as, 'People are our most valuable asset', the EMT concluded that people would be the basis of DBCT P/L's future success.

Congruency was now apparent between the EMT Operating Principles, the application of the principles of 'extraordinary leadership' and the key role that people would play in the realisation of the EMT's vision.

Implicitly another CSI was emerging - that of providing challenging growth opportunities for DBCT P/L people.

Interestingly, this vision would also form the basis of a sustainable competitive advantage for DBCT P/L. Competitors would find it hard to operate at the edge of chaos.

I have not mentioned the word 'trust' thus far. Healthy scepticism has received a mention, and given the previous initiatives visited upon the organization it was neither undesirable nor unexpected.

Elliot Jacques had been visited upon DBCT P/L with the benefit of establishing the requisite pattern of organizational strata. The Elliot Jaques journey however had a faltering start.

The Mutual Recognition Units (MRU's) established under the requisite pattern of organizational strata did, however, provide a sound basis from which to recommence our journey.

The conundrum of trust was that it was oftentimes viewed as being based on certainty. Certainty, in terms of the future, was not on offer. What, hopefully, was emerging was a consistency in behaviour exhibited by the EMT and the adoption, of those behaviours, by like-minded individuals within the organization.

Consistency of behaviour, based on the EMT's espoused Operating Principles, was seen as a sound basis on which to build trust. I mention the word trust at this time because the rate of organizational change and envisioned change being exerted by external forces on the organization, was starting to get seriously out of sync. The acceleration of change to position the organization would be radical and represent a risk both to the envisioned future and the individuals who were the guiding members of the organization. Trust therefore provided the glue for the EMT to embark on the next phase of the change programme and the only sustainable basis upon which to introduce a structured role review process for both maintenance and operations personnel.

Historically, both Terminal expansion and organizational change had been largely viewed as linear, albeit at accelerating rates. A period of exponential change, both in capacity and complexity, had been envisioned and was now rapidly approaching. In preparing for expansion, systems had been upgraded, training given and expectations of performance raised. A clear differentiation was emerging between those whose experience was of rote learning and those who had mastered process understanding.

Not only was this differentiation emerging, individuals were exhibiting signs of stress and some individuals, who now perceived a glimpse of the future, albeit veiled in mist, questioned their ability to contribute to the future. Acknowledgement of their contribution to the success of DBCT P/L and the ability to depart the organization with dignity was a heartfelt desire. As noted earlier there had been casualties both within the EMT and elsewhere within the organization as the envisioned future of DBCT P/L was both articulated and experienced. The ability to depart the organization with dignity was therefore a shared value.

The focus of the role review process was a structured assessment of top performer behaviour. The development of top performer behaviours was not the opinion of the EMT but based on input from DBCT P/L personnel undertaken in a structured and replicable workshop environment. The focus on behaviour and aptitudes permitted structured feedback to be given to individuals and the removal of the perception of bias. Individuals recognised that much of the basis of their future within the organization was dependent upon their willingness to participate and apply their talents.

The tapping of discretionary energy was to be a characteristic of the organization's future. Although not a pre-requisite for employment, living within an organization which sought to tap into discretionary energy was both an exciting and daunting prospect for individuals who exhibited a willingness to participate. Individuals were being given a choice with respect to their willingness to contribute to the envisioned future of DBCTP/L.

The role review process resulted in some 25% of maintenance personnel and some 40% of operations personnel leaving the organization. In a total establishment of 150, our journey had seen in excess of 25% of our people depart.

The emerging top performer behaviour required of a terminal system maintenance coordinator was that of team coach and facilitator. Technical leadership was not the only criterion. Coaching and nurturing the teams to permit the management to process themselves was a key organizational objective if the EMT's envisioned end state was to be achieved.

For this to happen, technical competency would no longer play the central role. Now, thinking skills, organizational skills, planning skills and diagnostic skills were valued more than the traditional 'nose down – tail up, fix it now' technical approach. Organizationally it meant that DBCT P/L was not seeking to sustain the mentality where, for example, it would produce the "worlds best gearbox maintainer". Those skills were best delivered by a specialist gearbox supplier. The focus was consistent with our maintainers being responsible for the process of maintenance. Contractors, in this environment were viewed as a flexible extension to maintenance, working for maintenance and therefore, industrially, not a threat.

The challenge of recruiting was onerous. The selection criteria applied was identical to that applied in the role review process and resulted in a strike rate of 5%. 800 applications were received and assessed, from several rounds of advertising to fill 40 positions.

The maintenance of the standards reinforced the integrity of the role review process since the final phase was the induction and training of the recruits by DBCT P/L personnel, some of whom were exiting the organization.

Although potentially a high-risk strategy, the engagement of individuals who were exiting the organization to train recruits provided an element of personal closure. In essence it was transparent to all that the top performer behaviours developed by the teams as part of the role review process were being honoured and that those people entering the organization were meeting that test. In addition, the aptitudes and experience brought into the organization meant both an accelerated learning curve and an enrichment of the talent pool. The transition witnessed by our departing employees gave them confidence that future success could be enjoyed by all.

It should not be construed that this scale of change can occur without disruption and some resentment. This resentment or tension provided a necessary energy source for change.
Let me take you back to the initial concepts of normal and extraordinary leadership.

Normal management was seen as being close to certainty and close to agreement. The change process impacting on DBCT P/L meant that although developed on the basis of certainty and agreement many of the aspects normal management, QA, safety systems, delivery and content of training, delivery and content of information systems were now not capable of providing a sound basis for DBCT P/L's envisioned future. The objectives of normal management, in the context of providing DBCT P/L a licence to continue to operate, had not necessarily changed, however the need to provide a basis from which to apply extraordinary leadership challenged the basis of their establishment.

If normal management systems did not change, much of the discretionary energy which we sought to tap into to achieve our future would be directed to fighting inappropriate rules.

Information and in particular how that information could be accessed and utilised, necessitated a complete review and ultimately the replacement of DBCT P/L's information technology and management systems. Although I have mentioned the role that departing personnel played in training new recruits, it should not be construed that the scale of change would not impact on the scope, content and delivery of future training and DBCT P/L normal management systems including QA, environmental management and safety management. A step change has occurred and if the envisioned future is to be realised the total integration of DBCT P/L normal management processes into the way we do our work is vital.

As was the case with the EMT during the strategic planning process, the top performer behaviour which would realise the envisioned future of the organization had moved from compliance to genuine commitment. Without genuine commitment the energy which was being tapped to achieve the increased terminal throughput would result in the EMT's harm and CSI's being eroded. In addition, society's assessment of the balance between wealth creation and consumption of resources had the potential to seriously limit DBCT P/L's future.

The phrase 'One Best Way' has been coined for this phase of the journey. In that process, knowledge and the sharing of information is deemed critical to the envisioned future of DBCT P/L.

Process improvement – all process – can only occur when there is consistency in understanding of expectation both across shifts and within the production and maintenance teams. This understanding will need the overt support of the EMT, and again will challenge the genuine commitment of the EMT to their operating principles.

Externally, the DBCT P/L business processes of 'coal chain management' and 'asset management' will form the basis of DBCT P/L's client's assessment of success.

The success of 'One Best Way' will underpin this critical business.

This phase of the journey has yet to be completed. However, trust, which underpins genuine commitment is strengthening during a period of increased hazard and incident reporting – the feedstock of improvement. Although an 'applied strategic planning process' had been developed and adopted by the EMT, there were periods where the focus on the process was downgraded and the production of a plan dominated.

This may seem strange in that having a plan gives the impression of certainty. As noted earlier, certainty was something the organization did not have and hence when the relevance of the plan began to be brought into question the EMT had nothing to fall back on. The process, the relationships, the trust, the broader leadership template, which the applied strategic planning process has given the EMT was not strong enough to permit operation at the edge of chaos.

The EMT members were therefore operating with less clarity outside the scope of the plan and the organizational decision making templates, which were a direct result of the process focus, were not always clear.

Tensions emerged within the EMT. The desire for certainty, at times was overwhelming. The desire to 'do' – in conformance to a plan – rather than think, coach, lead, develop relationships and trust was a very human reaction to the stress of continued change. Tensions emerged within the operations and maintenance personnel. Shift crews were recast. Friendships of many years were strained. This was an imposed change and, as in the case of those leaving the organization, the past needed to be honoured and those entering the organization given a chance to share and enhance their perception as to why the 'Terminal' was a special place. Following the role review process, the expectations of both new and old employees needed to be managed. Task skills were high on the agenda for new employees. All employees needed to be coached in the development of the new teams.

I am reminded of a statement of principle developed during organization planning for Green Fields Organization: '... the design of the 'process' belongs to management ... managing the 'process' belongs to the teams.' This succinctly re-states an EMT Operating Principle and in seeking to deliver on those expectations, the behaviours of the EMT and those with responsibility for the teams came under increasing scrutiny.

A number of key decisions were made:

- The inadequacy of terminal systems was becoming apparent and in order to provide information to maintenance teams managing the maintenance processes resources were directed to ensure data flowed to maintainers in preference to the EMT.
- Operations planning as a planning exercise was largely being set up for failure since, in a coal chain coordination role; planners were seeking to assume responsibility for things which were beyond their control. The focus of operations planning had to be integrity of data provided by participants within the coal chain and the process steps or elements within the Terminal which were to be managed by

the shift operations personnel. Shift performance was now to be measured by the effectiveness of the management elements of processes which occurred during the period of the shift – time was to be the measure not tonnes.

- The organization hierarchy was turned on its head with the organization depicted as the operations and maintenance teams being supported by Human Resources, Commercial and Strategic & Technical Development MRU's with the EMT providing the foundation of the organization. The Operations Planning group of the Commercial MRU now had a clear focus as to who their customer was – the production teams.

- The role of Production Superintendent was eliminated and the role of Manager Terminal Operations re-focussed to that of coach and facilitator. The shift production teams were:
  o clearly responsible for managing the 'process', and more importantly;
  o clearly responsible for meeting the expectations of the Terminal's customers.

The reaction of the shift crews was mixed varying from those who exhibited an attitude of, 'Hey guys it's our shift to work on; the Group Leader can't and I won't tell you what to do. We have to start to work as a team and work it out amongst ourselves' to 'What is going on here?'

Critically some tension had been created via an experiential learning intervention which created space for the teams to grow and reinforce the EMT's confidence in the teams to deliver. As noted earlier a key step in achieving a forward focus for the teams was the honouring of the contribution of both individuals and their teams to the success of the Terminal. The need and the strength of this process should not be under estimated in providing a foundation from which to tap into the organization's discretionary energy.

An integral part of the experiential learning programs, run prior to the role review process, was the opportunity for individuals to gain a greater insight into who they were, how others perceived them and the richness of their potential to the organization. The rate of pick-up with respect to task skills was accelerating and the need to manage expectations and develop willingness emerged. Given the focus of top performer behaviour in both the role review process and the subsequent recruitment process, a significant investment in ensuring our ability to tap into the organizations discretionary energy was now required if the full potential of the role review process was to be realised.

An initial reluctance to participate was apparent, in that probably in excess of 25% of participants of previous programs were no longer with the organization. Phase two therefore started tentatively; however, upon completion of phase three in excess of 90% of employees have attended. The course was not compulsory and sought to engage people on the basis of interest and word of mouth feedback. Interestingly, the nature of the course, which is an intensive week long residential activity has provided a shared experience for all of those who have attended – re-igniting the experience for those who attended the first series – and a code of silence such that those who have yet to experience the learning process will talk about the content but not the process, recognising that the process, out of context, would significantly diminish the value of the experience to future participants.

Having now spent a week with close to one hundred of the people who, for better or for worse, have found themselves joining me on the DBCT P/L journey, I must confess to being somewhat humbled by the experience. The depth of talent, the richness and diversity of experience of life that they bring to the organization creates yet an even greater challenge to deliver on the expectations arising from the envisioning process started by the EMT in 1997.

A critical outcome for all those who have participated is, I believe, a greater understanding and appreciation not only of themselves but of the richness and diversity that people bring to DBCT P/L. The journey has not had a singular focus of DBCT P/L's future but one of permitting individuals to start to understand and envisage their own futures. There will not always be a perfect fit between individual and organizational objectives. DBCT P/L's OMC contract expires in 2014 with no provision for renewal.

The EMT when asked to envision a future state for DBCT P/L drew people wishing to work and participate; people participating, growing and enjoying the experience; and people, having matured from their experience, leaving DBCT P/L for pastures new, confident in their ability to be successful in their new endeavours.

It is true that during the journey, the occasional panacea has been sought; however, there is no easy option other than consistency and commitment. The tools assembled and experiences gained are often extensive but the desire to seek additional easy fixes remains.

Upon reflection it is often easy to ignore those tools which were discovered early on but have fallen into disuse. The process for the identification of top performer behaviour and the identification of a process for 'Introducing Teams to New Ideas' stand out as simple, but effective tools which have assisted DBCT P/L.

Along the journey, external events have also influenced direction, probably the most significant being the Longford gas plant explosion in Victoria. Although not dealing with materials as volatile as gas, the forces in operation at the Terminal can cause significant damage to life and limb. The knowledge of process, as opposed to the learning by rote of process control, the management of risk and the creation of an environment of 'prideful wariness' have been reinforced by the lessons from Longford.

As an observation there remains an underlying concern that the one size fits all approach, which seems to have contributed to some of the problems of Longford, still pervades those who seek to assist organizations such as DBCT P/L. Safety systems, safety CSI's, quality systems and continuous improvement systems are often observed as being counter cultural and neither contribute to Normal Management nor the achievement of Extraordinary Leadership.

It should be noted that during the journey two significant external events have occurred;

- the negotiation of the Operations and Maintenance Contract; and
- the Leasing of the Terminal to Coal Logistics North Queensland

As an organization I think we have emerged from these events with greater confidence. Both were learning processes. The first was a considerable test for the EMT since life post-signature of the OMC was a real test of the envisioning process.

An observation would be that overall the organization faced the uncertainty of the leasing process with far more confidence, in that although there was no assured outcomes and minimal opportunity to influence the outcome, there appeared to be an underlying belief in DBCT P/L's capability, and hence their personal ability, to meet the challenge.

From a personal perspective, the journey with DBCT P/L has not been without risk. Confidence in my own ability to make a difference attracted me to the role in the first place. The challenges which emerged were markedly different from those which I had expected. My expectations were more in the area of the use of tools such as benchmarking, and the need to demonstrate the ongoing competitive position of the Terminal in a global environment. Not unexpectedly the challenges were seen as more cerebral as opposed to interpersonal. That latter is not an area many people enter into willingly without having first tested the water.

I would probably be the first to admit that I am a poor student of management theory. I am guided more by my experience and what feels right. What we have done and what we continue to do at DBCT P/L feels right. The risk, the investment in the human capital of DBCT P/L has been focussed on individuals finding out more about themselves and in doing so hopefully being liberated to want to make a contribution. No analysis, no incremental investment can provide either the certainty or the pilot to assess the validity of the underlying precept that people want to do a good job. The Board has given me the freedom. The EMT and the people of DBCT P/L have been prepared to participate. The fragility of the result can only be assessed when the answer to the question of what happens after I leave is answered. My reply has been that what we are doing together transcends any individual. If you want what has been created at DBCT P/L to survive, then it will –'if it is to be, it's up to me.'

# Notes

## MINERAL INTERNATIONAL
(a fictional name to protect the company's identity)
### David Napoli, 2003

### The Tension

We wish to share a story with you built on a real experience and it is one that applies to many different organizations.

### Background

The company is a moderately sized mining and mineral processor. It has an integrated process that mines the ore and processes that ore. The mines will be called P1 and P2, and the processing plants, P3 and P4. The work that we began was initiated by the general manager of P3.

P3 had a history of relatively poor performance and the company's executives took a decision to do something radical to improve P3's performance. They recruited a manager who had no experience in that industry and was not a chemical engineer, metallurgist or mining engineer. This appointment was a challenging and rather bold move. The person recruited to the general manager's position had a strong reputation for turning ailing businesses around and extracting extraordinary performances from them. In fact, the decision took that particular organization to the edge of transformation where new forms of operation were explored and implemented.

### The New Strategy

The general manager of P3 shared a simple philosophy about performance with us. To us, and to the company, performance has two components:

The <u>first</u> was **direction** and together we established a strategic direction to improve plant performance. The first strategy included *improving the reliability and safety* of the plant through improved systems and processes. The <u>second</u> strategy was to improve the *technical competency* of all employees. The <u>third</u> was to ensure all employees had the necessary *information* to ensure that the decisions made were in the best interests of the business. After all, there is not much point in developing technical competency and encouraging the application of those competencies, if people are denied the necessary business and process information. Without information, the application of technical competencies yields sub-optimal outcomes.

The <u>second</u> component of performance is **willingness**. Willingness is often overlooked since it involves working in the non-rational domain. Typically organizations spend a great deal of time and energy in getting the direction right and the creators of that direction assume that everyone in the business will follow with the same level of understanding and commitment. Most organizations hold that view. However, the general manager of P3 agreed that the assumption of willingness automatically flowing out of direction was invalid and agreed to work on securing willingness, or what is often called discretionary energy. A series of Extraordinary Leadership Programs (ELP) were conducted at the two senior levels in the business (P3) to ensure greater understanding and commitment to the strategic direction.

The general manager took an interesting and radical approach to those workshops. Rather than work with the executive team who showed considerable initial resistance to his personal approach to leadership and strategic direction, he chose to work at the next level (i.e. the superintendent level in that organization) and used the energy created at that level to influence the level above. The strategy was to give executive team members a new experience that would allow them to change their attitudes and approaches to improving the performance of the business. Experience had shown that concentration of technical solutions delivered through a command and control model had not been particularly successful.

Once support from the executive team was gained, a series of one-week residential ELP's were initiated. Those workshops were aimed at developing a strong commitment and passion for improving the performance of the business, with a reduced sense of dependency on management by the participants. Participation was an individual choice and volunteers came from all levels of the P3 business.

The workshops were chosen as the vehicle to initiate the cultural change. There was a long history of perceived alienation by employees and high levels of mistrust and dysfunctional behaviour. The workshops enabled participants to experience success through co-operation, win-win strategies and, provide the opportunity to work with pride – all in an uncertain environment. As result, participants went back to work with a deep desire to make a difference in the business and with an appreciation of how small changes can magnify themselves to achieve substantial outcomes.

It was necessary that the environment participants went back to was supportive of that wish to improve the performance of the business. This was not an environment that relied on heavy applications of external control and limitation. The general manager set about modelling the necessary behaviour and practiced high levels of inclusion with his team. That behaviour was mirrored throughout the P3 business after some little time. Fear and blame as a strategy was seen as unproductive and, in fact, the general manager constantly encouraged all employees to be 'free of fear and full of confidence'. What was important in that organization was congruency between the words, (espoused theory)[93] and the actions (theories in use). Only with congruency between actions and words would people develop trust and confidence in the organization and its leadership, and deliver that discretionary energy required for extraordinary performance.

The changes started to become apparent to other parts of the organization and they began to support the ELP's by sending people from their businesses to them.

## The Spread

Rather than attempt to change the whole business, the strategy of changing one part first was adopted. This is in fact how change was effected in P3. Now it was growing in the larger business in exactly the same way. Two of the remaining three general managers in the

---

[93] Argyris, C. (1989) *Reasoning, Learning and Action* San Francisco:, Jossey-Bass

business saw the positive results from the intervention and decided to enthusiastically embrace it. The third general manager (P2) chose not to embrace the intervention but, chose to focus on the development of technical competencies and systems to meet production needs.

One of the supportive general managers agreed to participate in one of the ELP's to gain a better understanding of it and what is required to support the investment that the business has made in that intervention. His participation sent a very strong symbolic message of support to the workforce at his site and those participants at that workshop reported a strong sense of alignment with that particular general manager. The other general manager (P4) remained supportive of the workshops both in terms of personal support and financial support by providing administration and actively encouraging participation by employees.

There was a recognition that if sustainable change was to occur in the business it would only happen when each individual made the choice to be productive, safe and happy. Therefore, the strategy was to work at the individual level. If an individual chose to be safe, productive and happy then other employees who came into to contact with that person would be obliged to do the same. That is because relationships are 50:50 arrangements, and we have no control over others, we can change others' behaviour only by first changing ours. They will then be obliged to change their behaviour in order to maintain the relationship.

The general manager of P3 and the other supportive general managers also believed that the difference between high performing organizations and the rest was the quality and quantity of information that flowed within the business. High performing businesses are those that have superior processes for collecting, analysing and disseminating information. To collect, analyse and disseminate timely, complete and quality inform-ation requires a culture based on trust and free from fear and blame.

**The Tension**

There were a number of events that stressed the business. Firstly, there was a change in the company structure that removed a significant cash flow from the business. Secondly, there were a number of technical failures and a planned major shut-down in P3 which severely restricted production. Thirdly, there was a management change that introduced an executive manager who seemed to be locked into mechanistic management and had very little appreciation of complexity theory. Rather than see the pursuit of extraordinary leadership as being based on sound systems theory, he and his colleagues probably thought that it was the 'soft and fuzzy stuff' associated with the old human relations school of management.

Being locked into mechanistic management drove 'command and control' behaviour within the business. The centralised control was underpinned by the belief that people in the organization were not willing to deliver total commitment to the business. In fact, people were seen as lazy. It was seen as the senior management's job to stir employees into action and to push them harder. There was also a belief that people could be frightened into higher levels of performance. This was at odds with the messages from the ELP's where it was clearly demonstrated that superior performance in integrated systems comes through cooperation. This created considerable tension between the general manager of P3 and his manager, the latter being driven by a totally mechanistic view of the business.

It also seemed that the organization was confused about the difference between leadership and management. Management is about maintaining what you have. Management is about control and limitation - the application of external controls and systems to limit actions. On the other hand, leadership is about performance. Leadership is the art of stretching the organization to achieve results that are extraordinary. It is about opportunities, innovation and growth. The general manager of P3 understood this but he was constantly assessed against his efforts in mechanistic management, rather than the assessment being broadly based to include his leadership successes. The confusion between management and leadership was, and still is, a source of considerable tension.

At the plant level, most of the general managers were attempting to show genuine leadership, balanced with appropriate management, whilst the corporate office was attempting to exercise mechanistic management. In reality, both management and leadership needed to be exercised by the corporate employees. This is an illustration of the tension that arises at the point where mechanistic management and extraordinary leadership meet. At this point judgement is required but it is actively discouraged. Failure to exercise judgement, or to allow judgement to be exercised, continues to drive the organization to mechanistic management where the prescriptions are clear and unambiguous. But is it useful when the organization exists in an environment and market place that is far from certainty and therefore, far from agreement as to what decisions need to be made and what actions need to be taken?

A more fundamental tension is the challenge that quantum physics has presented to the Newtonian thinking that 'haunts the corridors and board rooms of most of our corporations'[94]. The bureaucratic nature of organizations is being challenged by the theory of complex adaptive systems. Newtonian thinking sees the organizations as a series of linear relationships with simple cause and effect outcomes. The company and its senior executives are desperately trying to hang on to this Newtonian thinking even though the evidence suggests that it is an inappropriate paradigm from which to build a high performing organization. The company's financial performance reflects its 'limiting' management strategies.

Complexity theory, on the other hand, sees organizations as a set of relationships that are governed by non-linear feedback loops. The consequences of seeing organizations through the 'quantum lens' is that individual actions become amplified both positively and negatively to deliver unpredictable outcomes. Those outcomes could exceed the organization's wildest expectations. Again, this tension is played out in organizations when the executive is wedded to the fantasy of control from above and predictability, (that is the bureaucratic relationships) as opposed to the base of the organization, which lives with high levels of uncertainty and values responsiveness. Responsiveness is not seen as a failure of predictability.

At a micro-level we saw this tension played out. In each of the plants, strong emphasis was placed on production planning. Production planners sent their plans to the shift managers to set the shift targets and activities. Planners by definition strive to achieve certainty and their work comfortably fits in the realms of mechanistic management. Shift managers, however, live in a work environment that is far from certainty

---

[94] Youngblood, M. (1997) *Life at the Edge of Chaos: Creating the Quantum Organization*, Richardson, Texas, Perceval Publishing.

and often, at the edge of chaos. Nature does not distribute the ore as predicted by the geologists, stockpiles do not contain the quantity and blend of ore shown by the planners in their schedules and equipment unexpectedly fails. This is the scenario faced by the shift managers. Therefore, it is easy to understand why the shift manager treats the production plan with cynicism and contempt. It was evident that relationships in the company were often strained, as a result of people working on different objectives and using different approaches. For planners, predictability is valued. For shift managers, responsiveness is valued. What is crucial is that both share information with each other to improve each others' performance and understand the framework in which each is obliged to operate. The manager of P3 understood this and worked to improve the relationships and information between the various functional groups. This work was not understood and valued by the senior management who chose to see only through the mechanistic lens, a lens that relies on rational and logical processes only.

There are two other points of tension in the extraordinary leadership model. The first is at the point where the organization operates in the belief that it is close to certainty and close to agreement. People are often asked to do things that they know are not in the best interests of the customers and owners of the business but honour the bureaucratic requirements of the business. Here employees feel a sense of helplessness and hopelessness and decide that the business is heading down the path of failure and extinction. Their strategy is to get as much as they can from the business before it eventually dies. They may also see the business as 'morally corrupt' and choose not to commit to a business that they believe does not deserve to exist. At this point they play the game of negative politics – take advantage of others, deceive others, withhold vital information, provide misleading information, etc. The tension here is debilitating. The manager of P3 recognised this point of tension and the associated common response to plant issues – 'who gives a .....'.

On the other hand, the tension that exists at the edge of chaos is invigorating. Here people are energised by the challenge of achieving extraordinarily but they know that there is a risk of failure. People are focussed on achieving extraordinary results and not behaving politically. They are drawn to work with others and seek comfort and safety from them as they attempt to achieve results that have never been achieved before. Here the political behaviour is positive and built on the basis of co-operation, inclusion and encouragement. This was, and continues to be, the strategy chosen by the general mangers of plants P1, P3 and P4.

## The Results

The story began with P3, so let's go back to it. During the period when both mechanistic management and extraordinary leadership were exercised, we understand that the business was able to achieve its business targets despite having two major plant failures. Employee turnover was reduced and anecdotal evidence suggested that employee commitment to the business had reached levels not experienced in the past. Sufficient trust had been developed between employees and the company to enable the establishment of a new set of non-award contracts of employment.

The management team achieved a sustainable improvement in performance by recognising and facilitating small changes in the daily activities of individuals. The team adopted a management approach that was based on the sound scientific principles that underpin the theory of complex adaptive systems. In doing so, there was a reduced sense of dependency on those in hierarchically senior positions to take action. Quicker responses to problems and potential problems were obvious and the information flows were far more comprehensive, reliable and rapid. This looked like a recipe for a committed and productive organization.

Unfortunately, and frustratingly to us, the appointment of the executive manager along with his mechanistic management style, has now filtered down through the organization and has challenged the earlier initiatives of developing an organization based on the ideas of complexity theory.

The general manager of P3 has moved on to be CEO of a new organization and it will be interesting to observe developments in P3 over the next few years. Will it continue to grow and develop based on the model of extraordinary leadership or will it regress to a command and control mindset with a focus on limitation rather than a focus on performance and growth? The fundamental question for the executive is, 'Does it really want performance or is it interested only in control?'

Chapter 13

## MANAGING CHANGE WHICH BENEFITS ALL
## Geoff Voigt Manager, Rolling Mills, 1999

The last seven years has seen BHP Integrated Steel Whyalla Operations' Rolling Mills manage the introduction of significant equipment and technology improvements that have delivered major efficiency benefits for the Department.

These changes include:

* A major upgrade of the electrical system to facilitate the rolling of cast feed;

* New roll and schedule designs for all product sections;

* Significantly improved reheating practices;

* The design and commissioning of new sections to improve export and domestic market competition;

* The installation and commissioning of automated Cooling Beds;

* The introduction of the operational control L3 system and

* Decommissioning of facilities at the Soaking Pits, the Bloom Mill and the Bloom and Reconditioning Yards.

The benefits delivered as a result of these changes include:

* A significantly improved safety performance with the Department's Lost Time Injury Frequency Rate (LTIFR) reducing from 66 to 2, and 1,000,000 hours worked lost time injury free;

- A 155% increase in Mill capacity from 400,000 to 620,000 tonnes per annum;

- A delivery rate consistently over 95% and

- A 35% reduction in maintenance costs.

These benefits have been more remarkable given they were achieved in a climate during which a significant down-sizing of Rolling Mills personnel was pursued. This saw a more than 50% reduction in the Rolling Mills workforce.

Critical to the successful introduction of equipment and technology improvements has been the continuous planned focus on involving people in the management and implementation of these changes in order to achieve Business Plan goals.

ROLLING MILLS MODEL

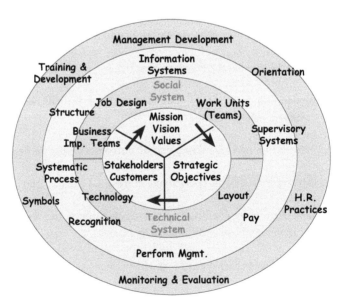

Figure 13.1 Change model presented by David Napoli

## The Rolling Mills Vision

The Rolling Mills Vision was developed to articulate the future goals in terms that described the future work environment. It also responded to the frustration that some people had in understanding the Department's Business Plan strategies and actions.

The introduction of major automation and a new rolling process and section designs in 1991 were complex initiatives. It soon became apparent that our people were not clear on the direction of the business and its goals, or their place the scheme of things. They had little sense of ownership of the actions for which they were responsible. People could not visualise where they fitted in. They understood, however, that non-achievement of goals would impact on their daily work and their long term future through the Rolling Mills' continued viability.

The first draft of our Vision described the process, automation, its impact on people, strategies for the involvement of employees, potential technology changes and strategies for improved safety performance.

All Rolling Mills' employees were involved in discussions aimed at increasing their awareness of the direction that the Rolling Mills was taking. These sessions were critical to providing employees with information and time to discuss, amongst other things, the implications, their roles and planned equipment and technology changes.

For the first time all Rolling Mills' people were able to share a common view of what we were all working towards. The operators, support staff and management could visualise the goals and had a picture of the future as a basis for continued discussion. We could now see where we were inconsistent with the Business Plan Vision and what needed to change to meet that Vision.

Our actions for the last seven years have been driven by this work and the main parts of our Plan were realised at the start of the 1997/98 Financial Year.

## Involvement Programmes

The involvement of our people was achieved by the use of rational processes in which all could be involved. From this involvement came the building of teams that were typically cross-functional in make-up, with Supervisors providing leadership for Maintenance and Production Operators.

The focus of these programmes was to provide well-defined tools, skills and techniques which employees would utilise to achieve clearly defined goals. Whilst these processes were resource and time intensive, they were very useful and continued to meet the Department's technical problem-solving needs.

We learnt a number of important things from this involvement programme.

We found that employees were often 'press-ganged' into attendance at meetings and did not follow through the stage of formal decision making. We sought their involvement because their ideas were recognised as valuable but we did not involve them in the final decision making.

Systems to identify issues and problems, and actions to resolve them were necessary to keep the teams driven towards their goals.

But, we found that successful team involvement was more than people armed with rational process tools meeting to discuss a number of issues. Effective team relationships with a clear purpose driven by the broader Vision, Values and Business Directions were also essential.

## Teams Today

The development of teams as they are today has been an ongoing and emerging process over the past two years and will continue to be so. We have continually questioned and measured our practices and existing structures against our Vision and Beliefs about how we do and should work.

It should be noted that the Rolling Mill leadership team discussed and decided that we were not aiming to develop 'self-managed' teams – they may emerge some time in the future. The aim was to develop mature groups that could openly and easily function, utilising information to make good decisions on how they achieved the business targets. There was a large amount of learning for most groups to move to this point. Throughout this time only one small group approached the self-managed position, where group members took responsibility for their business through activities such as their safety planning, budgeting and negotiations with suppliers.

The technique of Ongoing Critical Reflection has enabled us to recognise and deal with inconsistencies between *what we say we are going to do and what we actually do*. This challenge continually confronts us all.

The Organization Development Manager, Daphne Hart, has supported the design and development of this work, as an integral part of our Business Strategy. She is a member of all teams helping to provide direction, skills development in the context of work and observation of the teams' ongoing facilitation.

The development of a Leadership Team with shared commitment and common understandings and expectations has been essential to supporting the development of teams across the Rolling Mills.

Some significant steps that have been taken include:

- The involvement of Team Leaders in Steel Leadership Programmes to increase their skills and understanding of the leadership skills required to support the Mills developments;

- The development of a set of agreements described in behavioural terms to direct and monitor our individual actions;

- These are carried by all of us as reinforcement of our commitments and are used as a reference if our behaviour is inconsistent with that agreed. We have reviewed and developed these over time as circumstances have dictated;

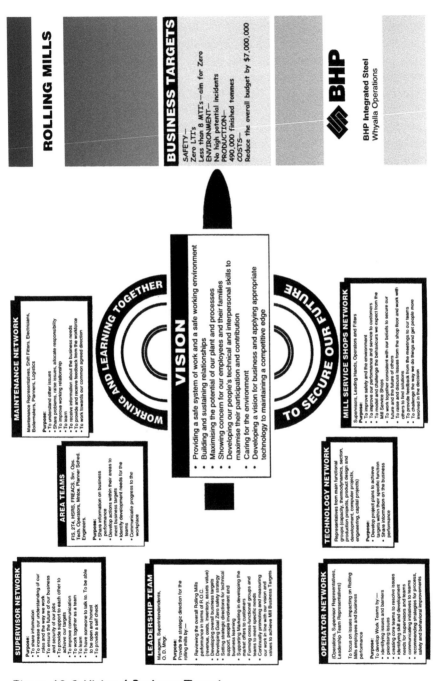

Figure 13.2 Vision / Business Target

- Holding regular weekly meetings to encourage issues to be put on the table and to increase our understanding of other's perspectives and barriers to the achievement of our Business Targets
- Acknowledging that some people in the support staff or management area could not understand or work to our agreed values and vision and
- Forming support networks, often at peer level to openly discuss how we achieve the goals required and how we support the operations.

**Supervisor Network**

Critical throughout this process has been our review of the role of our supervisors and how they were placed to achieve our planned directions. The Leadership team believed that within our organization and culture, the supervisors played a critical role. The role required modification to focus more on support and learning, but was essential. Supervisors were experienced, talented and well developed in hierarchal control. They often knew the answer without the need to involve people - focussing instead on reactive as opposed to pro-active processes.

Almost all shift and day supervisors attended Steel Leadership Programmes. This gave supervisors the opportunity to understand leadership concepts and, importantly, learn about themselves, their workmates and their work relationships. This developed common frames and language on which our work was based and escalated the development of our teams.

The Supervisor Network, comprising 16 supervisors, the Mills Management Team and the Organization Development Manager, met every three weeks.

We began by recognising the good work that had already been achieved by supervisors and the diverse role that they played, whilst challenging them to also understand the implications of their new direction and the individual commitment required of them. Developing a shared understanding about how that may look was an important step.

Supervisors were asked to describe how they, if they were the Plant Manager, saw a successful Rolling Mills in three years time. They shared their visions and from this we developed roles and responsibilities and operating values. We agreed also that we would provide regular, simple feedback to employees on their performance. Feedback was made systematic and a process to ensure consistency was developed.

Whilst the Network Meeting is informal, a check-in ensures we are all fully present and creates the Agenda for the session. The check-in process is a powerful tool used in many of our meetings. Issues raised cannot be ignored and almost always must be resolved by the entire group. We discuss, debate and problem-solve together until we find a solution that is acceptable to all and consistent with our Vision and Values.

The Supervisor Network has developed into a more pro-active team. Members are more prepared to confront issues within their group as an alternative to the 'blame management' approach of the past. New leaders have emerged and the group demands and challenges the members who do not participate. They see themselves as responsible Co-Leaders in the Rolling Mills Business.

This group has played a major role in shifting the work groups focus on to the Business. Their understanding from these network discussions has been applied and deployed on shift - with rapid results.

### Lessons Learnt

- As teams mature the person, or persons, responsible for making a decision must be identified. More and more people will want to make decisions, but at times hierarchal leaders may have to make the final decision. The level of decision making must be made clear at the start.

- The Supervisor is always seen as the leader of the work group and can strongly influence the results achieved.

- Supervisors need support to begin to challenge old habits and behaviours that we have previously accepted.

**Operator Network**

Whilst the Supervisor Network was being developed we called for representatives from across the Rolling Mills to join a session aimed at sharing improvements and workplace change, successes and needs. The group developed its Purpose, Operating Value and Meeting Format. Coming together to meet enables employees to discuss current issues as seen by the work groups and encourages people to take ownership of and work through improvements without support. The reaction by those willing to try something different has been good. As individuals and work groups learn about costs, regulations and systems their perspective changes. Whilst they see why some things cannot be done overnight they also challenge existing inefficiencies. The new expressions of anger at 'BHP getting ripped off by suppliers' is refreshing.

Work groups launched several small activities to save costs. Operators would deal directly with suppliers, and management would smooth out the systems to remove barriers and support them to get results. The operator network took on jobs such as painting the large office area themselves; another group landscaped about 70 metres of land that not only acted as a roadway safety barrier restricting access and proving better control, but also greened-up the area. All of this has been achieved at little cost. Employees relocated the dirt, bark chips and irrigation systems from other projects through direct negotiation. They persuaded a contractor to supply surplus bushes from an external contract for free.

The operator network progressed into Area teams as a concept, which in turn progressed into developing the natural shift teams. This was negotiated as part of a new workplace agreement, with the aim to further develop the overall team and maximise people's exposure to the business performance and issues, and concepts such as meeting check-ins and operating to mutually agreed behaviours.

*Lessons Learnt*

- Unlearning old models of control is a slow process with even those enjoying a success ready to slip back to the old ways if things got tough.
- There is a fine balance between offering support through this Network to allow different behaviours and the new belief that the 'Operator Network will get it done'.

- The initial drive to pursue something different comes from the willing few prepared to have a go.

### Area Teams

We are looking at the further development of Natural Shift Teams. These teams have clear identities and developing relationships, but with group sizes of about 20 per Supervisor they will require careful monitoring.

Whilst we develop the skills required for this to be successful we have introduced the concept of 'Area-based' teams. Each area of our process has been identified and production operators, mechanical and electrical engineers, maintenance planners and shift maintenance people assigned. A shift technical specialist facilitates these teams.

Management has set broad targets that are primarily safety and capacity related at the moment but will develop into whole-of-business targets. How these targets are achieved is largely up to the teams to manage, as long as they operate within the Rolling Mills' Value system and Vision.

These teams are in their early stages of development. With enthusiasm the teams meet each week, but as we work a four week roster cycle this leads to changing membership - an issue that had not been contemplated.

To facilitate the teams' growth a health program has been introduced - facilitated by a group of consultants from a company called Restart. This not only provides health knowledge and improvement but also provides a common focus with a degree of self-disclosure of fears relating to health issues. The team members construct their own programme and help each other achieve individual goals. No subject is taboo. People want to understand how to manage stress, their weight and cholesterol and (for our mainly male workforce) the issues of men's health.

The initial group from Materials Handling has already shown a very marked reduction in sick leave (both in total days and especially in the number of absences greater than one day).

The Area Teams are providing a vehicle for close interaction with the technical group, who were often criticised in the past as being 'office based'. Our most successful Engineers demonstrate that they are good listeners and constantly check with the work groups throughout the design process. They use their skill to complement the idea, not replace it with something better. They are beginning to work as Process Consultants.

Communication, listening and learning skills are becoming the key to success in maintaining working relationships that achieve business targets.

### Lessons Learnt

We allowed the teams to meet as they needed. A strong desire to get going and involve all four shifts meant weekly meetings with often-changing memberships. This made team building very difficult. Key groups and people were not attending.

The technical and maintenance day people quickly began to develop new relationships.

### Maintenance Network

The Maintenance Group has been faced with difficult targets to reduce maintenance spending, whilst at the same time increasing reliability and availability of the process and equipment that has grown in complexity. There has also been increasing dependence on Contractors and the reduction of spares. For most of our history, maintenance has been celebrated for their speedy recoveries after unplanned breakdowns. Now, they are confronted with a small work group and very tight cost controls to achieve record availability targets. Preventative Maintenance has become the focus.

Understandably, the group struggled with what were seen as conflicting targets between Breakdown and Preventative Maintenance. The Maintenance Network was formed to clearly communicate expectations and business needs and to enable employees to express their views. Maintenance shift personnel, planners, supervisors and management were each represented.

A Vision of a perceived future to meet these increasing demands was drafted firstly by the maintenance superintendents and then presented to members of the whole group who added their stories. The group developed its own slogan to capture their Vision:

*'Rolling Mills Maintenance team are expert predictors and planners and learn from breakdowns.'*

Whyalla Operations<br>
BHP Integrated Steel

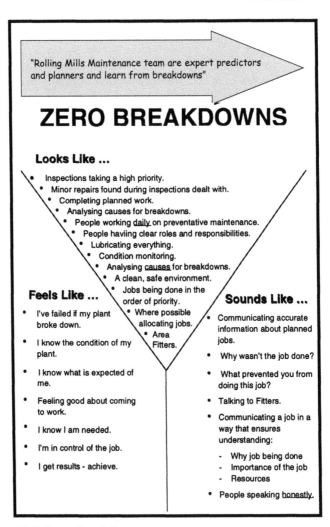

Figure 13.3 Zero Breakdowns

A key aspect has been the development of explicit descriptions of the behaviours required to achieve the Vision. These are displayed throughout the Rolling Mills and are used to monitor developments.

Whilst the group is at an early stage of its development, it is still demonstrating both increasing understanding of business demands and a willingness

## Managing Safety in a Changing Culture

There is a very high priority and focus on safety, with ever diminishing targets as we head towards the goal of zero accidents and injuries.

Our safety focus is integrated with and cemented by our developing workplace culture.

Our start was mainly with setting standards and confronting those who wanted to step outside the values of the Rolling Mills team. We learnt that people had to remain clear that Management was responsible for and would set the standard. We invited discussion, developed trials where applicable and used question/answer sessions to develop understanding and boundaries. Auditing and involving people to check their understanding of the reasons behind the rules was used.

There are a number of significant events in the Rolling Mills Safety Story.

About five years ago one of our people was electrocuted at work by a defective plug - a single strand of copper wire. We set up a special group to systematically hunt down every form of risk on electrical equipment. The group made excellent achievements but while this work progressed, we reached a turning point when we understood just how often electricians were getting 'tingles' - an 'undiscussable'. At that time five new young electricians transferred to us. Statistically they would have a shock soon and were at the greatest risk. Despite our efforts and warnings, one by one, they reported shocks.

John Searle the Maintenance Superintendent tried a different approach. He had several people talk about the electrocution - the deceased's friends, workmates and his young wife told their stories.

Following this input, they wrote on a card the names of people that depended on them and their safety. These were printed and produced on A5 cards for the group to carry with them as reminders of their stake in acting responsibly.

Each of the recent shock recipients talked about their incidents. A change occurred. They no longer blamed the old equipment but talked about the behaviours and the responsible actions they needed to take to ensure their safety and the safety of others.

At the beginning of 1998 the maintenance group had several serious injuries from very minor incidents. Simple trips or stumbles on walkways resulted in broken bones. There was nothing to re-design. There was no technical solution.

This has led us to explore what drives behaviour - the balance of consequences that lead to taking a specific action. We are describing the positive attentive behaviours we want to observe and are currently using anchors to these behaviours.

Maintenance is now modelling their Safety Meetings on our Network Meetings. The Agendas, largely formed from the check-in process, are exploring the true beliefs of the work group as we look towards our Goal Zero target.

**A New Challenge**

The Rolling Mills proudly achieved the productivity and safety goals in late 1998. The productivity targets were maintained consistently for six months demonstrating their sustainability. Records were frequently re-written.

By October '98 the impact of the Asian crisis was undeniable. The technology team led by Ian Ottaway quickly developed many new sections to meet international standards as we sought new market areas throughout the world, but eventually falling currencies and international politics meant that we could not maintain the throughputs that Rolling Mills was now capable of achieving. With a minimal export market for the foreseeable future the 7 day- 4 shift roster could not be sustained, impacting heavily on the potential earnings of the people and on the competitiveness of our product. Job losses would occur as we restructured the business, and inventories were climbing at an unacceptable rate.

People had been kept informed of the situation and were aware that our options had closed. To deal with this problem a two-day workshop was constructed, involving union organisers and union delegates from the four unions, a representative from each shift and workgroup and management. The objective set for the group was to

> 'Deliver the business targets in terms of safety, costs, quality and market, and in doing so, provide the best solution for the people.'

The organiser of the union with the major membership supported the approach, and together we met with the group each day to understand what they had worked on, and see if union and management could live with their ideas. The group quickly raised new ideas on work practices, understanding that if there were benefits to the company they may be able to accept more work, and hence reduce the gap in their potential drop in earnings.

Examples included production people helping do maintenance work. We typically had 1 day per 4 weeks where we stopped production for 24 hours and maintained the plant. Production operators were rostered off, and large numbers of maintenance contractors were employed to do the work. The proposal was for production people to assist, utilising reason-able levels of skills. Groups of 3 or 4 production people would be led by a tradesperson. This greatly freed the trades people to utilise their skills, and allowed production people to understand their equipment. Even cleaning up was changed so the focus was on cleaning and inspecting, providing more reward to those doing the task. It was calculated that this would save about $200,000 per annum. This was a difficult proposal to realise. Production was fearful that management would replace unskilled people with trades people, and equally the trades people believed management's intent was to rid themselves of their group.

Coupled with this concept was a time bank approach, which allowed the groups to effectively bank time that they exceeded budget rates. This eliminated unnecessary inventory build-up, and provided a positive pay incentive to achieve the overall targets.

The group was responsible for detailing their concepts and communicating the ideas back to their workgroups. After the work was completed, they coordinated a secret ballot for overall acceptance of the proposal to ensure everyone's view was captured. When the site management and unions gave the approval, a six month trial agreement was put into place.

### Lessons Learnt

- The Rolling Mills group demonstrated they were able to change their paradigms, debate, discuss and work together towards a common goal. They respected the boundaries set, and fully utilised the site's resources to be able to meet a new challenge to their normal lives.

- The new agreement was seen as a new foundation to changing they way we worked together as a business and opened new levels of trust between all groups.

### Summary

Whilst we continue to meet new challenges, our strategic approach, based on the business targets, our vision and values, and the focus on learning enables us to work together to find solutions.

**We continue daily, to learn new lessons.**

## THE METROPOLITAN CEMETERIES BOARD
### Peter MacLean, CEO, 2002

The Metropolitan Cemeteries Board in Perth, Western Australia is a statutory authority appointed by the State Government to manage designated cemeteries in the State Capital. The Board comprises seven members from various disciplines and is currently responsible for the management of five operating cemeteries and three crematoria. It is developing a new memorial park at Rockingham, a rapidly growing urban area south of Perth.

The MCB also has a planning role in terms of providing for future cemeteries and crematoria and provides advisory services to Cemetery managements throughout the State.

The Board receives 8800 funerals per annum at its facilities.

The total number of staff over all sites was 103 (at the time of writing.

In 1988 the name and charter of the Karrakatta Cemetery Board changed to Metropolitan Cemeteries Board. The new Board was charged with the responsibility of managing Pinnaroo Valley Memorial Park (formalising a previous arrangement of management by the same people under a separate Board entity) and new cemetery land at Baldivis was vested with a government commitment that it would be developed as a replacement for the East Rockingham Cemetery which was fast reaching its capacity for burials.

Operationally, Pinnaroo had functioned autonomously to a large degree and it was necessary to commence changing the culture and structure to reflect the new metropolitan wide responsibilities.

The government also indicated that the Board was to have a planning role advising the government of the day on cemetery site requirements and early in the life of the new Board, the management of cemeteries at Midland and Guildford was transferred to Board jurisdiction.

The organizational structure was basically hierarchical starting from a Manager of Operations and a Manager of Administration at Karrakatta and an Operations Manager at Pinnaroo.

A variation was tested at an early date whereby the Pinnaroo Manager became Landscaping Manager with responsibilities over all of the cemetery sites.

An early imperative was to computerise all of the cemetery records. Karrakatta and Pinnaroo records had previously been keyed into the central treasury mainframe system with microfiche available for perusal at the cemeteries. That facility was no longer available and so the Board needed to undertake a data conversion and design, and develop a suitable system with all records from the turn of the century and cross reference to reflect all transactions on graves and cremation memorial plots.

With demands to upgrade the old cemeteries inherited, commence planning and development of the new site at Baldivis, co-ordinate and upgrade existing operations and develop improved facilities at Karrakatta and Pinnaroo and keep pace with modern technology and promotion of a customer service focus, support staff at a higher level than the leading hands was necessary. Supervisors / coordinators were progressively introduced in areas of need, i.e. landscaping, funeral services, information technology, client services and human resources.

It was apparent in the administration/client services area in particular that the growth and complexity of the organization required management at a higher level than the traditional cemetery administrator, and a Manager of Corporate Services was appointed to oversee financial, information technology, human resources and the whole of government corporate services. This was growing at an alarming rate, and with both the FAAA (Financial Administration and Audit Act) and Public Sector Management Act conferring greatly increased responsibilities.

It became apparent that responses to the rapid changes outlined above had in some areas not been adequately co-ordinated and another imperative was for a properly developed strategic plan with clear goals. A workshop to address the strategic plan, organizational structural issues, communications and culture was conducted and facilitated by David Napoli. All managers and co-ordinators and a cross section of the general workforce were invited to participate in the workshop. A comprehensive SWOT analysis was part of the program.

It became apparent, partly through poor behaviour during the three days of the workshop, that there were dysfunctional elements. It certainly clarified for the CEO where obstructions were occurring both in terms of communicating policies and vision downwards and particularly in taking advantage of the confidence, energy, dedication and creativity of staff below the second level of management.

The Chief Executive Officer noted that particularly in the areas of human resources, client services and landscaping, very competent co-ordinators were increasingly frustrated by the inability to progress reforms and efficiencies and cultural changes to get the best out of good people within the organization.

In at least one other case a co-ordinator with ability but who was poorly managed became counter-productive as she endeavoured to bypass lines of authority and withdrew from communicating adequately and constructively. It was also apparent that whilst core business activities were being reasonably planned and addressed there was a lack of corporate development and planning and probably a general lack of corporate focus. Including and beyond the examples above, roles, responsibilities and accountabilities required clarification and there was a need to design jobs to achieve organizational objectives. There was some evidence that jobs had been designed to meet personal needs.

There were other influences at that time with government encouragement of competitive tendering and contracting and outsourcing of at least non-core services. Internally we recognised the increased need for marketing and commercialisation, the need to improve our community education function in terms of bereavement and the services the Board provides, and the rapidly developing opportunities for increased benefits from information technology.

The Board commissioned a review of organizational structure addressing these and other issues.

The revised structure created a flatter organization devolving decision-making authority and accountability to the lowest possible level.

Importantly, and on the recommendation of the Human Resources Manager, Carolyn Baldwin, new job description forms for all positions would highlight the fact that everyone had a responsibility for, and would play an important role in customer service. Senior positions in the organization have responsibilities for strategy, policy, planning, consultation and collaboration and the less senior positions in the hierarchy have a responsibility for participation, implementation and ownership. To accommodate this we adopted a matrix structure with customer service focus the overriding consideration. Shared participation, implementation and ownership across the organization would ensure that individuals do not become solely focussed on the achievement of the objectives of their functional groups.

The concept of a learning organization was also important in the cultural change to be achieved beyond the implementation of the new structure. This means that in the organization:

- *Information is generated from multiple sources*, through wide-spread scanning and collection of internal and external information;
- *This information is integrated into the organization,* through having open access and no secrets;
- Through using the richness of multiple perceptions, *collective interpretation is reached* and
- *Authority to take action* is held at the appropriate level in the organization.

Great importance would be placed upon achieving a shared vision across the organization.

We decided that a Corporate Council would be established with the six line Managers, Director Corporate Development and the Chief

Executive Officer. It should be noted that on the original analysis there were three different levels related to the work value of each of the management positions and yet at Corporate Council it was to be clear that no Manager was senior to the other, nor did the Director Corporate Development 'have stripes'.

Early meetings were interesting in that the senior of the Managers in the old hierarchical structure clearly did not believe in the flat structure and his body language and behaviour at Corporate Council meetings brought this out. Nor was he supportive of the expanded consultation processes throughout the organization and believed that the Manager's job was to manage and bring order to the operations.

As a group we persisted with the consultative and collaborative concepts and the Manager experiencing difficulties resigned. In another area there was constant unrest and suggestions that staff could not complete their duties satisfactorily, because there were not comprehensive procedure manuals guiding every action. Further, the cemetery records system (a comprehensive burials and cremations database) required many changes to be effective and operational difficulties were not being dealt with properly. These were given as reasons for dysfunction in the client services area.

When a new Manager was appointed to Client Services with an extensive background in cemetery administration and the computerised database, it was soon apparent that neither the lack of a procedures manual nor the shortcomings of the computer system were the real problems – it was really poor management, lack of motivation and training and a constant search for excuses. Most importantly, improved leadership brought out the best in the staff.

Five years beyond this experience, comprehensive procedure manuals are not in place, only guidelines and encouragement of flexibility and initiative to meet the diverse needs of the community we serve. Similarly, the computerised cemetery records system is fundamentally unchanged and meeting organization and client needs. With eight people on the Corporate Council (management group) having ownership of their position and responsibilities in a small organization it was immensely important that we considered the manner in which we would work together.

As a legacy from the past hierarchical structure, a fair bit of work would be necessary to promote a shared vision and clear understanding of the interdependence of all within the organization. This suited the style of the CEO where empathy means thoughtfully considering employees feelings along with other factors in the process of making intelligent decisions. The relationship extends to full disclosure to the Board and staff, no secrets and openness in all dealings.

The values developed collaboratively within the organization are as follows.

We are committed to:

• striving for customer service excellence through continuous assessment, innovation and improvement;

• acting ethically with integrity, professionalism and courtesy;

• providing a safe and caring workplace where people can achieve with pride;

• trusting, supporting and cooperating with each other and the community and

• caring for our environment – past, present and future.

Our shared vision is compassion, respect and understanding as we pursue our mission to provide quality services and facilities for burials, cremations and commemoration.

As indicated earlier, to operate successfully with a flat structure and have all stakeholders buying into the shared vision it was important to establish a climate of mutual respect and trust. We tried to develop a constancy and consistency in this area, giving clarity to what was valued and to be stood up for. It is difficult to build and maintain trust if actions and values are constantly moving. This is difficult to achieve when the working environment and external factors are changing so rapidly, and it was also necessary to build comfort with ambiguity and openness to change.

An example which brings out the real complexity of the environment in which we work is that on the one hand we are a government agency required to comply with FAAA, the Public Sector Management Act, State Supply Policy and a host of other rules and regulations, whilst on the other hand we receive no contribution from consolidated revenue and are required to operate on commercial principles.

Operating on commercial principles requires creativity and in the case of cemeteries management a delicate balance between marketing and commercial initiatives and community service obligations and sensitivity for the bereaved. We engaged David Napoli as a facilitator so that we could collectively address the issues involved in meeting what we loosely called the 'blue areas' of our charter, i.e. the regulations or our licence to operate and the 'green' which required us to reach out and operate on the edge of chaos.

As a group we have fairly successfully achieved within this paradoxical environment. As time has gone by a further spin-off has been the benefits of out of the square thinking in the blue and the green areas - the stark differences are not as apparent as they used to be. A recent example was the desire to present a gift to a long serving employee in line with Board policy. The cost to the Board would effectively double with the imposition of fringe benefits tax. There were also Public Sector Standards issues. The Human Resources Manager suggested that the gift be in the form of an additional contribution to the employee's superannuation, a solution appealing to the employee and not penalised under the Commonwealth Fringe Benefits Tax legislation.

We endeavour to involve people in the organization to the maximum degree and ensure that views can be expressed without fear or favour. Beyond the day-to-day inter-relationships and communications we encourage an open door policy and regular forums such as the Workplace Consultative Committee where issues can be raised and ideas developed. Certainly every endeavour is made to disseminate all information widely.

Another influence on the way we have worked together is encouragement to follow the *Seven Habits of Highly Effective People* as set out by Stephen Covey.[95]

### Habit 1 - Be Proactive

We encourage all to accept responsibility for their own actions and to work and improve continuously within their circle of influence. We have largely succeeded in developing a culture where people do not blame others when things go wrong but work together to resolve problems. The CEO has often said that if decisions and actions, and the processes in reaching them are fair and logical based on proper motives then employees will be supported even if something goes seriously wrong.

We encourage continuous improvement and provide opportunities for personal and organizational growth.

### Habit 2 - Begin with the End in Mind

We endeavour to offer principle centred leadership and focus more on people than things, and through developing relationships have succeeded in getting most employees to buy into the shared vision and objectives.

### Habit 3 - Put First Things First

Processes are in place to clearly establish organizational priorities at all levels. Whilst this is difficult with always competing priorities, the matrix and duty statements focusing on customer service as mentioned earlier generally ensures that high priority activities receive attention and more timely and significant effort.

### Habit 4 - Think Win-Win

This is particularly important in the sensitive field of our endeavours. We have established strong relationships with stakeholders and

---

[95] Covey, S. R. (1990) *Seven Habits of Highly Effective People: Restoring the Character Ethic* Melbourne Victoria, the Business Library.

partners in service such as the funeral directors. Again it comes back to interdependent relationships with mutual benefits for all concerned – particularly the customer.

All of our key processes are consultative, seeking out win-win. When there has been a perceived need for structural changes all, or the relevant section, of the workforce is involved. At the time of budgeting and other stages of planning, consultative and collaborative processes apply.

## Habit 5 – Seek First to Understand, then to be Understood

This comes back to empathy and empathetic listening. We have come a long way from misunderstandings and mistrusted motives and points of view. We have gone from large egos, advancing own ideas, defending positions, attacking contrary opinions, etc. to really seeking a clear understanding of others points of view, needs and ideas.

As an organization we share feelings, emotions and sensitivities.

## Habit 6 – Synergise

This works on the basis that the whole is greater than the sum of its parts and in this organization a great deal of work has been done on empowering management and every employee in an environment of trust and open communication. We have gone a long way in recognising interdependence internally and externally.

There are many examples of creativity, improvement and innovation well beyond individual capacities throughout our organization and facilities. A few examples would include our cemetery records system on a website, the first and most advanced multiple use cemetery reserve in Australia at Pinnaroo Valley Memorial Park, sand mining at Baldivis Cemetery to generate revenue and create correct contours, a cemetery redevelopment program at Karrakatta, leading the nation in cemetery sustainability, the Infants' Butterfly Garden, an Employee Relationship Development Plan which is being used as a model in the public sector, etc.

## Habit 7 - Sharpen the Saw

Again this comes back to the learning organization and the need for continuous improvement as well as providing training opportunities in a formal sense. We have endeavoured to provide adequate support systems, organizational identity through the provision of uniforms and social interaction through a subsidised social club as well as staff breakfasts and other opportunities to meet together.

We would like to think that we have provided transformational leadership creating the frame of reference within which transactions take place. We have endeavoured to change the minds and hearts of the people and organization towards a great vision with clarity of purpose, clear values and challenged by change.

Principle centred and transformational leadership has brought out some of the following qualities:

- releases human potential;

- recognises and rewards significant contributions;

- identifies and develops new talent;

- makes full use of human resources;

- aligns internal structures and systems to reinforce over-arching values and goals;

- is preoccupied with purpose and values, morals and ethics and

- builds on personal needs for meaning.

There is dignity, meaning and community in the workplace. We have developed a holistic view involving many people with differing views and perspectives.

It is true to say that all human emotions reflect in a workplace and emotions such as humility and humour are important in the sensitive field of our activities. As our Landscaping Manager has often remarked, 'If we stop laughing we have a problem.' These words were spoken at very difficult times in the organizational transformation but it is another facet that we have endeavoured to encourage – a happy workforce and workplace.

## INDEX

For Product Safety Concerns and Information please contact our EU
representative  GPSR@taylorandfrancis.com
Taylor & Francis Verlag GmbH, Kaufingerstraße 24, 80331 München, Germany

www.ingramcontent.com/pod-product-compliance
Ingram Content Group UK Ltd.
Pitfield, Milton Keynes, MK11 3LW, UK
UKHW021607240425
457818UK00018B/428